All Abot
Poetry

The East

Edited by
Angela Fairbrace

This book belongs to

First published in Great Britain in 2010 by

Young**Writers**

Remus House
Coltsfoot Drive
Peterborough
PE2 9JX
Telephone: 01733 890066
Website: www.youngwriters.co.uk

Foreword

At Young Writers our defining aim is to promote an enjoyment of reading and writing amongst children and young adults. By giving aspiring poets the opportunity to see their work in print, their love of the written word as well as confidence in their own abilities has the chance to blossom.

Our latest competition *Poetry Express* was designed to introduce primary school children to the wonders of creative expression. They were given free reign to write on any theme and in any style, thus encouraging them to use and explore a variety of different poetic forms.

We are proud to present the resulting collection of regional anthologies which are an excellent showcase of young writing talent. With such a diverse range of entries received, the selection process was difficult yet very rewarding.

From comical rhymes to poignant verses, there is plenty to entertain and inspire within these pages. We hope you agree that this collection bursting with imagination is one to treasure.

Contents

The Poems

The Sky

The sun has fun lighting up the sky,
We can watch the birds fly by,
At the end of the day the sun says goodbye
Ready for the night to begin.
The moon is bright,
When it's dark at night.
As far as you can see
The stars shine all over me.

We have rain, snow and frost for a reason
They gather up for every season.
The clouds make rain to water our garden again.
The blue sky and the sun make our holidays lots of fun.
The sky is great, and I can't wait
To see what tomorrow brings.

Sophie Dennis-Horne (8)
Dale Hall Community Primary School, Ipswich

Autumn Time

Autumn - cold,
Leaves falling down,
Coloured leaves,
Trees, tall and small,
Fireworks,
Snipply, snap and *bang!*
Fishing by the cold greeny lake,
Looking for some floppy fish,
Bonfire Night, a favourite time,
Cannot see in pitch-black!
Storing apples red and green,
Ginger beer!
Autumn - a fun time of year!

Shannon Harvey (7)
Dale Hall Community Primary School, Ipswich

Summer

Hot summer, smelling lovely
Flowers in the breeze,
Walking in the squidgy grass,
Watching birds fly high in the sky!
Going to the beach, sunbathing,
Standing on the sharp shells,
Bike riding down the hill,
Seeing butterflies fly from bush to bush.
People having fun, fun, fun!

Charlie Williams (7)
Dale Hall Community Primary School, Ipswich

Sunny Beaches

The scorching sun shining on the hot houses
And reflecting into the rippling water,
Sunny days on the yellow beach,
Waves splashing on the steaming sand,
Put your snazzy costumes on and jump into the warm pool,
Ice cream time for hungry tummies.
Summer is here, summer is here!

Aimee Back (7)
Dale Hall Community Primary School, Ipswich

Happiness

My happiness is the pink of the sunset,
It tastes like a ripe red strawberry,
It smells like baking bread,
My happiness looks like a field of gold,
It sounds like loud pop music,
My happiness is the perfect thing for me!

Isabel Cadwallender (8)
Dale Hall Community Primary School, Ipswich

Fear

My fear looks like a sharp knife,
It is as black as mud,
It smells like burnt sausages,
It tastes like rotten bread,
It feels like hard rice,
It sounds like a raging car alarm.

Jacob Bailey (9)
Dale Hall Community Primary School, Ipswich

Excitement

My excitement is as bright as glossy white snow dripping down,
It looks like a double, extra bouncy trampoline going *boing, boing,*
It feels like an amazing clown tickling up and down my body,
It tastes like a massive, delicious, giant burger with tomato ketchup,
It sounds like loads of people cheering for Ipswich winning,
It smells like tasty, fresh fried fries sizzling in an unused pan.

Maddie Wegg (8)
Dale Hall Community Primary School, Ipswich

Spring

Spring has warm weather and
The summer is on the way.
That little bit of drowsy rain
Again and again.
Everyone having a new start,
Spring is fun! Fun! Fun!

Sam Rawden (7)
Dale Hall Community Primary School, Ipswich

Anger

My anger looks like a shiny red pepper
It smells like rotten eggs
It tastes like a burnt potato
It sounds like a monster roaring
It feels like a hard rock.

Harrison Hadley (9)
Dale Hall Community Primary School, Ipswich

Autumn

Thundering fireworks in the cold breeze,
You can't get to sleep,
Lots of colours on the giant trees,
Walking through the damp woods,
The sun reflecting into the dark river.

Zac Gissing (7)
Dale Hall Community Primary School, Ipswich

The Funky Zoo

F unny animals, I love it!
U nhappy? So go to the zoo,
N o bad things there.
K ing lions you will see.
Y ou will love it.

Z ebras are lovely at the zoo.
O uch! You can get hurt.
O ooo, wow, it is so nice because it is cool.

W ater time, splash around
O rang-utans are cheeky
W eather does not matter.

Sophie Green (8)
Edward Worlledge Community Junior School, Great Yarmouth

Sporting Disasters

Bats and balls
Absailing falls
Too long grass
The trophies
Made of brass!

Quad bikes's broken
Lost your hiking
Token

The captain's
Sick on cricket
Day, oh no! I
Broke the wicket
No way!

The rugby pitch is
Wet so I brought my
Pet pig

The captain wears a
Wig, he is bold
I was told.

Hannah Bensley (9)
Edward Worlledge Community Junior School, Great Yarmouth

Dragons

D reading being slain
R ampaging around on the hard, cold floor
A lways on the run
G one in time
O ctopus tentacle-like tail
N ever trustworthy
S ad but true that they are extinct.

Ebony Geddes (8)
Edward Worlledge Community Junior School, Great Yarmouth

Jodie Brand

J elly is yummy in my tummy
O ranges are sour and have lots of pips
D addy is playful, I play with him a lot
I love my mum
E very day I go to school

B ingo is fun, Mum loves bingo
R unning is good for you
A pples are yummy
N uggets taste nice
D ogs can be any colour.

Jodie Brand (8)
Edward Worlledge Community Junior School, Great Yarmouth

Good Movies

G ood movies are worth watching
O ptimus Prime is my favourite character
O n goes the movie and let the action begin
D ad likes horror movies.

M onsters and aliens make an awesome movie
O ff-roading movies are cool as well
V ampires are in lots of cool movies
I ndiana Jones is awesome
E ndings of movies are bad because the movie has to end
S ad movies are boring - action and adventure are the best.

Joseph Bircham (8)
Edward Worlledge Community Junior School, Great Yarmouth

Skateboard

S kateboarding is cool
K eep up
A t the park it is fun
T ony Halk is a fantastic skater
E veryone knows
B am is also a good skater
O n the ramp it is fun
A re you hurt?
R un as fast as a skateboard
D iving up and down the ramps.

Hadleigh Brown (9)
Edward Worlledge Community Junior School, Great Yarmouth

Fairy Dust

F airies live in little tree houses
A round when we are sleeping
I have blue and pink fairy dust
R ushing around so that we don't see them
Y ellow flowers in their lair.

D oing all the fairy dust for children
U nder my pillow a tooth is waiting
S uch a small house in the trees
T here is all sorts of fairy dust.

Bethany Ellis (9)
Edward Worlledge Community Junior School, Great Yarmouth

Monsters - Haiku

Vampires and old ghosts
Zombies coming out their graves
Black spiders and bats.

Samuel Webb (9)
Edward Worlledge Community Junior School, Great Yarmouth

Snowboard

S liding through the thick snow
N o chucking snowballs in the race
O ver and under the bumps in the snow
W ater melting when winter finishes
B oarding under bridges
O ld men watching
A re you stuck in all this snow?
R unning around to get to the race
D ying for winter again.

Zac Ralph (8)
Edward Worlledge Community Junior School, Great Yarmouth

Birthdays

B e happy on your birthday
I 'm going to be ten today at midnight
R oller skating on my birthday
T alking to your friends
H ow do you feel now you're ten?
D o you like your cake?
A birthday only lasts a day
Y ou will be ten all year
S ad because you want a birthday every day.

Chantelle Fulcher (9)
Edward Worlledge Community Junior School, Great Yarmouth

Lego Models

L ovely coloured bricks
E normous models made out of Lego
G reen bricks make brilliant grass
O paque bricks.

Andrew Poole (8)
Edward Worlledge Community Junior School, Great Yarmouth

Swimming

S wimming in the swimming pool is fun
W aves come on sometimes
I love the swimming pool
M um is taking me swimming on Wednesday
M y brother splashes me
I zoom down the slide into the water
N oisy children swimming happily
G iant waves splash against us.

Olivia Dinsdale (9)
Edward Worlledge Community Junior School, Great Yarmouth

Swimming

S cuba-diving is fun
W aves push against us
I watch a swimming show
M y mum helps me in the pool
M y dad gets me soaked!
I love the smell of the chlorine
N oisy children swim happily
G iant waves crash against the side.

Melissa Whiting (8)
Edward Worlledge Community Junior School, Great Yarmouth

The Letter

In the morning I got a letter at 3am
I got out of bed, I fell downstairs and I opened the door
What was there? A golden letter with a golden stamp.
I wondered, *what is it? Is it the bills or the Billy Jean CD*
I opened the letter, what did I see?
Oh no, not the bills! Oh really! Just give me my little break!

Keenan Pallett (8)
Edward Worlledge Community Junior School, Great Yarmouth

Monkeys

M unching on bananas
O n trees hanging from their tails
N aughty monkeys throw coconuts
K eep away or they will go bananas
E very monkey has a tail
Y ou will have to come and see them
S wing from tree to tree.

Kieran Cunnington (9)
Edward Worlledge Community Junior School, Great Yarmouth

The Hairy Dog

The dog is hairy with spots, but just loves logs.
His bed is made of logs!
His best thing in the whole world is rotten apples!
He stinks just like my dad's socks.
Hairy with fleas jumping round like a circus.
His tail is as long as a trunk.
But I'd say he's as wobbly as jelly!

Taylor Ellis (8)
Edward Worlledge Community Junior School, Great Yarmouth

Reanna

R ainbows shine like the sun in the sky
E lephants eat peanuts with their trunks
A bright red rose is my favourite flower
N ever eat Brussels sprouts but save them all for me
N aughty children get told off, it isn't very nice so be good
A bowl of cereal is not my friend because I spill half every morning.

Reanna Storey (9)
Edward Worlledge Community Junior School, Great Yarmouth

School

S chool is boring
C hildren to discover
H ome at last when the day has done
O utside at playtime
O ff for six weeks in summer
L essons are messy and fun.

Katie Drury (9)
Edward Worlledge Community Junior School, Great Yarmouth

Homework

I put my homework in my sandwich
Homework is like a big, fat, slimy piece of meat
It's slimy like bogeys
I hate homework
I think I'm getting poisoned!
Can we start again?

Billy Laffitte (8)
Edward Worlledge Community Junior School, Great Yarmouth

About Me

C onna is my name
O utstandingly funny
N ot always nice
N early really good
A pples are good.

Conna Robertson (8)
Edward Worlledge Community Junior School, Great Yarmouth

Snake

S lither along the rough ground
N ever make a snake angry
A re you scared?
K angaroos stand on them, *squish!*
E ating humans if you are unlucky.

Travis Probert (8)
Edward Worlledge Community Junior School, Great Yarmouth

Snake

S limy snake
N asty snake
A mazing snake
K ing snake
E lectrical snake.

Tyler Wiseman (8)
Edward Worlledge Community Junior School, Great Yarmouth

Nightmare

Nightmare, indecisive,
Where shall he go?
Knocking gently at the carved wooden door.

The door creaks open,
Slams against the wall,
Nightmare wakes
And lurks.

Nightmare lights up thoughts,
Blocks of moving colours,
Swirls and spirals,
Twisting his brain.

Albany Hodgson (11)
Emneth Primary School, Wisbech

The Ginger

Zingy, tangy as pure as a lemon,
This ginger smell that must have come from Heaven,
Fresh and mouthwatering, the best smell ever,
But this smell's always brilliant, unlike the weather,
The smell is like a cold ice cream on a hot summer's day,
This smells as rare as the white clean snow in the middle of May,
Beneath the knobbly, wrinkly skin,
Some big as an elephant, some small as a pin,
Yellow moist, you will find,
That picture of ginger you won't get out of your mind!

Jasmine Dady (11)
Emneth Primary School, Wisbech

Wind

The wind is a howling devil.
Pushing and pulling at fences and trees.
As invisible, powerful enemy.
Moaning and groaning around the chimney pots.
Howling like a coyote in the highest mountains.
Swirling and turning high and low,
Taking leaves along as it goes.
Watching as the clouds dance swiftly by.
Then suddenly, as quick as it entered,
The wind had finally stopped.

Martine Harvey (10)
Emneth Primary School, Wisbech

Light

Light is like an angel,
Flying through the planets,
Lighting up our world.

Light sneaks up on the darkness,
With its sword of lightness,
Blinding the evil, scary monster.

Light is a creator,
But also a killer,
What would we do without light?

Joshua Hammond (10)
Emneth Primary School, Wisbech

Darkness

The darkness is like the thief
Stealing the sun,
The sun is afraid of dark,
It's pitch-black
Like black ink pouring all over my work,
Darkness swirls around people like an invisible cloak.
At sunrise he scatters away,
Where does he go? . . . Nobody knows.

Ellie Broomfield (11)
Emneth Primary School, Wisbech

Nightmares

Nightmare, she follows you in the darkness,
Hiding in the darkest of shadows,
She takes over your dreams,
All you can hear is her screeching and howling,
Your heart will pound when a nightmare is near,

So *beware,* never ever stay up too long!

Rachelle Lubi-Hallam (11)
Emneth Primary School, Wisbech

The Ball Of Happiness

The sparkly breathtaking ball of happiness,
Glistens above me on the best day of the year,
His friends are with him but he stands out the most,
And he is the one who doesn't like to boast,
His sparkle glistens like the stars above,
And like I said he's the one who stands out the most.

Madeleine Melisa Deneri (11)
Emneth Primary School, Wisbech

The Sunny Sphere

Golden sphere,
Shining like a sun on a sunny day,
Turning like a dog chasing its tail,
Shimmering as it turns, patterns,
Vine-like trees in the forest,
Like a ballerina dancing.

Shannah Wiles (10)
Emneth Primary School, Wisbech

Cars

Racing down the motorway as fast as it can go,
Pumping petrol through its pistons,
Backfiring as it goes,
Wheels gleaming,
Paint shining,
Just like it's brand new.

Jack Maryon (11)
Emneth Primary School, Wisbech

Winter Wonderland

The snow fell like a blanket covering the countryside
As the ice sparkled like a diamond in the cold breeze.

I stared around, mouth open, I couldn't believe my eyes.
The scenery was a wonderland, magical in all sorts of ways.
I crept forward, instantly a snowball smacked me
Right in the face like a bee sting,
I threw a snowball in the sky,
It soared like a rocket on a mission.

Slowly I looked up to see a new batch of snowflakes
They tickled my skin like a feather duster.
I stepped again
I got greeted by a new boulder of snow,
It felt as cold as an ice cube in the fridge.

All of a sudden little kids came out to play,
Building snowmen and falling around hopelessly,
'Aah, I hope this never ends,' I whispered to myself.

Sooner or later the snow started to vanish,
The happiness faded and everything was normal.
I was still excited about . . .

Christmas!

Jessica Rachael Edgeley (11)
Fakenham Junior School, Fakenham

Jack Frost

Jack Frost sends armies of hailstones
To sting our bare faces.
Gales and blizzards start to have
Icy snowflake races.

Fluffy snow closes around us
Sealing us in our home,
It's too cold to go outside,
We're enclosed in a dome!

He knows that we see him
As an imposing figure,
Even so he sets to work
With surprising vigour.

The biting wind whips the trees
And brings travellers down
To their knees.

Jack Frost has grabbed the Earth,
And doesn't want to let go,
But the world is calling springtime
And is fed up of his snow.

The hibernating animals pray
In their sleep for life,
And the trees hope and hope
For the end of their style.

Georgia Bottomley
Fakenham Junior School, Fakenham

Winter Comes

The snow is a blanket over the earth.
The ice is a window on the ground.
Winter is as bitter as a lemon.

Jordan Crook
Fakenham Junior School, Fakenham

Snowfall And Cold

Slowly and calmly,
The snow gets deeper and deeper,
Each day,
Each night,
Each hour.
The children go and play,
They don't like to stay at home.
The snow is like white diamonds,
Scattered across the concrete.
As people walk around the valleys,
They get the feeling that the snowmen are staring
At them, with their coal eyes.
Lots of people don't like winter,
They say that they are freezing cold,
But I think that they just exaggerate.

On the other hand, some people love winter,
They feel all excited and glad.
But once it goes they all turn sad.

Rosie Lawlor
Fakenham Junior School, Fakenham

Hello Jack Frost

J ack Frost nips at your nose
A snowman stands proudly out in the snow
C old air dances around
K ids leave footprints in the snow

F rost lightly blankets the houses
R obins fly around the winter wonderland
O n the ground and the trees, snow slowly vanishes,
S pring is here
T ime to say goodbye to Jack Frost.

Danielle Bird
Fakenham Junior School, Fakenham

The Cold, Cold Winter

The snow is like an apple crunching beneath my feet
It looks like a white blanket laying across the concrete.

Children are getting excited, as Christmas is nearly here
While mums and dads are relaxing, drinking nothing but beer.

Christmas trees are up with beautiful decorations
Kids are out playing, joining the celebrations.

Hibernating animals roll over in their sleep,
Bears grunt and growl, but from rabbits not a peep.

All around the land, bells begin to ring,
As carollers start to sing.

Santa Claus and his reindeer are on their way,
Little boys and girls can't wait for Christmas Day!

Alisha Cooper (10)
Fakenham Junior School, Fakenham

Winter World

As winter comes the snow falls like a blanket
Covering the countryside.

As I watch it sparkle from the sky above
I see the clouds move slowly across the sky.

The ice is a diamond shimmering
In the cold breeze.

As I sit at my window
Watching the snowballs flying through the air,
I stare at the scene, it is like looking at a magical winter
wonderland.

I see the patterns of snow angels printed into the crunchy snow.
Sadly as Christmas comes, winter goes.

Danni Steward (11)
Fakenham Junior School, Fakenham

Winter Wonderland

The Christmas bells are ringing
Everyone is singing
When winter is in town.

Mince pies are coming out,
The children scream and shout,
When winter is in town.

Santa is coming here,
Parents drink some beer,
When winter is in town.

Everyone shouts with glee,
Around the Christmas tree,
When winter is in town.

Kirsten Cunningham
Fakenham Junior School, Fakenham

Snow Girl!

Cold as ice.
Gigantic as a mountain.
Chubby as a newborn baby.
Sleeping, still, silent, striking like a fashion
Model posing on the catwalk.
Smiling as if she won the war.
Yet as soft as a teddy bear's fur.
Quiet as a senior citizen frozen with sadness
When one has died.
Her face as sweet as sugar.
Trees drooping with jealousy at the snow girl's face.
Yet her face sick with all the fans bowing over her day and night.

Hannah Reed
Fakenham Junior School, Fakenham

Snow

Snow harder! Snow more!
Snow blizzards galore.
I can't get enough of
This fluffy white stuff.
Snow! Snow! Snow!

Snow a ton! Snow heaps
Snow ten feet deep.
I wouldn't cry if it
Snows till July!
Snow! Snow! Snow!

Katy Ferris (10)
Fakenham Junior School, Fakenham

Winter Chills

Winter chills everyone's feet
So birds no longer come out and tweet
Hedgehogs curl up in a spiky ball
Squirrels scurry about for their lost acorns
Cars sail across the frozen ice land
People come out and greet the giant snowman
Spring comes
The changes begin.

Niamh Thompson (10)
Fakenham Junior School, Fakenham

Winter

The snow is a blanket over the earth.
The ice is a cold mirror on the ground.
Icicles fall from the sky.
If you listen you may hear them shatter on the ground.

Joeb O'Hanlon (11)
Fakenham Junior School, Fakenham

Winter

Phoenix fire bird in a hot place,
Burning the village down.
A battle with the best warrior,
Amazing crimson, fire bird.
Terrified as winter starts to snow, hail and rain.
They all scream, 'The monster's dead!'
But when winter thought it had won,
Spring came round and beat the one.

Sean Whitesides
Fakenham Junior School, Fakenham

Winter

W is for the wind whispering silently in the air
I is for icicles like daggers waiting for the kill
N is for naughty or nice, whether you get a Christmas present
    from Santa
T is for tinsel, a decoration you put on your Christmas tree
E is for entertainment to go out in the snow and play
R is for Rudolph, his nose as red as a cherry.

Daniel Youngs (11)
Fakenham Junior School, Fakenham

Winter

W is for whispering, the trees whisper in the coldness of winter
I is for icy, like your breath is surrounding you like a glass dome
N is for that nasty cold or bug you get every cold winter
T is for tinsel, the decoration you put up at Christmas
E is for eager as the children are eager to play in the snow
R is for receiving presents from Santa.

Daniel Smith
Fakenham Junior School, Fakenham

Winter

W ind starts to whistle
I ce starts to form
N ew Year is coming
T ime for Christmas
E xcitement starts
R eindeer jingle in the midnight sky.

Tyler Armiger (11)
Fakenham Junior School, Fakenham

Winter

W ind starts to turn, strong
I ce starts to come as the snow arrives
N ew year is coming
T ime is for Christmas
E xcitement starts to happen as the snow comes
R obins start to fly.

Demi Karli Beck
Fakenham Junior School, Fakenham

Winter

Flying the Earth on icicle wings,
Using her roar she blows vicious winds across the Earth,
Winter looks for her weak and unsuspecting prey,
Taking up the reins, Spring comes and ruins her rampage over Earth,
Slinking back to her grotto,
She desires revenge for Spring.

Kira Dawson (11)
Fakenham Junior School, Fakenham

Winter

Winter is a destroying beast,
As white as ice.
Its growl fills the air and makes all shiver,
Winter desires the world to be cold
And dark.
It lives in the darkness of mountains.

Alexander Angus
Fakenham Junior School, Fakenham

Don't Be Such A Bully

Don't be such a bully,
Cos you kick and you punch me.
Me and my friends don't like it.
Don't be such a bully!

Bethany Moxon (10)
Fakenham Junior School, Fakenham

Summertime

S   ummer breeze
yo U   and me together
M   um cooks a fresh batch of cookies every day
M   y aunt Muriel came with us to go to the beach
E   vening time cold can be very cold
R   *uff* is the sound my dog makes in the morning
T   ypical are my afternoons
I   n Cromer I go to arcades
M   y cousin takes me to town every Saturday
E   xcellency comes from the heart.

Katy Murphy (9)
Great Cornard Middle School, Great Cornard

The Seaside

The seaside is never too hot,
Never too cold, it's just right!
It's not too dry, not too wet, it's normal!
Not full, not empty, in the middle
Lots of people go there with their children
To play in the sand and sea.

Jasmine Lindon (9)
Great Cornard Middle School, Great Cornard

Fireworks In The Sky

F lames on the bonfire crinkling
I n the night sky all bright and full of colours
'R ather delightful,' the posh people say
E verybody jumping, hip hip hooray
'W ow,' say the crowd with so much excitement
O ther people don't enjoy it as much as each other
R eading a book under their black and white cover
K icking and punching that's what brothers do
S haking and holding your mum's hand, called Sue.

I n the
N ight sky

T he mixed colours flow
H ey, that man's got an Afro
E verybody gazing at the dark sky until *boom!*

S pirals and curls
K iller swirls
'Y ay,' they all say

Jay Mallett (11)
Hainford Primary Partnership School, Hainford

Winter's Alive

As I walked out
On a crisp winter morn
The trees' fingers waved at me,
All tattered and torn.

The benches joined in,
Smiling at me.
Their neat wooden planks
Straining to see.

Gravel on the path
Danced along.
The little ones singing
Their beautiful song.

As I reached the door
The doorbell winked.
I felt slightly embarrassed
And my cheeks pinked.

Grace Mellows (11)
Hainford Primary Partnership School, Hainford

My Favourite Place

My favourite place
Is my room
It is ever so new
Because the bed has been moved

My room can be cool
It makes you want to drool
But don't get fooled
Because it is phenomenal

Even though the hamster rattles in her cage
But that doesn't bother me now!

Daniel Porter (10)
Hainford Primary Partnership School, Hainford

Lion Pride

Racing to their wildebeest prey
The cubs know that today's the day
With no food, they starved for a week
Food is what they will now seek
Lionesses call out to tell food's about
As flocks of cubs do not pout
Then out of the blue there comes a great *roar!*
Then all the lionesses back down to the floor
Then they scatter and let the mighty lion eat
He feasts on his own while cubs wait in the heat
Lionesses wait in the bush, they sit and pout
They wait till he's finished and till food's about
When he's finished, they eat and eat
The pride will now not retreat
They scoff their faces till it turns dark
Then fall asleep on a near tree's bark.

Alex Le Mesurier (11)
Hainford Primary Partnership School, Hainford

Pets

Cats are clever
Dogs are fast
Rabbits jump
Hamsters spin.

Dogs are as fun to play with as a rabbit
Cats are as clever as a robot
Rabbits can jump as high as the sun

Cats are cheeky
Dogs are athletic
Rabbits are playful
Hamsters go round and round.

Matthew Germany (9)
Hainford Primary Partnership School, Hainford

The Tennis Ball

As the ball flew by
Shooting to the ground
Bouncing up and down
Splashing in the pouring rain.

Crashing towards the ground
The ball started screaming
Sharp stones pointing up
Wanting to grow tall.

He'll never see his soul
Touching the ground
As he wanted to hear a sound
Nearly falling through a hole

The tennis ball was going to crash
And just wanted to stand.

Scott Johnson (10)
Hainford Primary Partnership School, Hainford

The Monster And The Mouse

It was a stormy, stormy night,
A monster woke in a fright,
Saw a mouse on the floor
Then chucked him out the big front door.

The mouse said, 'Oh please let me in,
Otherwise I'll have to sleep in your dustbin.'
'I don't know,' said the monster to the mouse,
'I don't like mice in my house.'

The monster can't sleep,
Without his cuddly sheep,
Does the monster like the mouse at all?
No! Because he's playing with his favourite ball.

Olivia Hill (8)
Hainford Primary Partnership School, Hainford

Pretty Much . . .

P retty poppies all dainty and red.
R ats are dirty and make me feel dead.
E ndless trees give a jolly wave
T here at the beach, the tedious adults bathe
T ummies gurgling 'cause dinner's ready
Y achts out at sea, they just take it steady.

M ums and Dads are caring and kind
U seless my life is, but I don't mind
C oncerts are fun and unforgettable
H ad a good game and I pretty much . . .

Loved it!

Katie Grimmer (11)
Hainford Primary Partnership School, Hainford

Dance Like A Tiger

Dance like a tiger when it
Just got its prey

Jump as a kangaroo
On a normal sunny day

Stalk like a grey cat
That's aiming for its supper

Scuttle like a squirrel
Collecting nuts

Snap like a crocodile
With lots of cuts.

Francesca Le Mesurier (9)
Hainford Primary Partnership School, Hainford

An Animal Alliteration

Wonderful, whirly whale
Slimy, splashing starfish
Tough-tempered tiger
Zigzagging zebra
Bitter, buzzing bee
Great, grumpy gorilla
Dangerous, daring dragon
Mega messy monkeys
Rough, refusing rhino.

Sydnie Snowling Dunford (11)
Hainford Primary Partnership School, Hainford

The Animals

I am a great big monkey much like you.
Swinging on the vine as fast as you.
The elephant clomping on the pavement
Making the biggest sound ever.

The long, long giraffe with his really long neck
And the little ant who is so small
That you can't even see him.

That's what I like about animals.

Rebecca Gunton (8)
Hainford Primary Partnership School, Hainford

Swim Through The Ocean

Swimming through ocean
Blending in the background
Doing all the things fish love doing
Blowing bubbles as they go
Minute by minute, sucking on the coral.

Leestefan Drake (9)
Hainford Primary Partnership School, Hainford

Shooting Star

I watched the silent stars so bright,
As they twinkled through the deep, dark night.
As they twinkled through the deep, dark night,
I saw a brilliant moving light.
I saw a brilliant moving light, a shooting star,
A wondrous sight.
A wondrous sight in the deep, dark night.

Helena May Mellows (8)
Hainford Primary Partnership School, Hainford

Ben, Ben

Ben, Ben, I am ten
And I steal pens and lots of hens

Then I get Ben and then
I get a pen
I then eat the pen

And there is a pen in the den.

Andrew Howes (8)
Hainford Primary Partnership School, Hainford

When The Rain Came

It was a cold, wet day,
As the raindrops slid down the windows,
Joy turned to sadness,
Laughter turned to sighs.
People hurried to find shelter,
Pulling up their hoods as they ran,
Rabbits disappeared into their cosy burrows.
Squirrels scurried to their nests.
When the rain came, sadness took over.

Sofia Hammond (10)
Herington House School, Brentwood

Appointments

I have a busy week ahead,
Dates and times buzzing in my head!
I have appointments everywhere,
Am I supposed to be here? Am I supposed to be there?

Monday at nine it's dentist time,
Hopefully my teeth will be free of grime.
My teeth are as white as fresh falling snow,
Thanks to the Colgate toothpaste I know.

Haircut on Tuesday,
I'd like to have my hair in a different way.
Head back in the sink
Shall I have my hair dyed pink?

Wednesday I'm off to the surgery,
I hope there's nothing wrong with me!
I have such a bad headache,
Maybe it's because I've got more appointments to make!

Thursday is the day of my eye test,
Which will help me see the best.
The optician said to me,
'Now, look at the letters, what can you see?'

My favourite appointment is on Friday
Pampering, pampering all the way!
A facial, a massage and pink shining toes,
A day at the spa, and my whole body glows.

It's Saturday and I'm going to put my feet up
And drink hot chocolate out of my trendy pink cup.
One thing I know for sure
I won't book a week like that anymore!

Hannah Spicer (10)
Herington House School, Brentwood

California

California, the golden state,
Its beaches glimmer
And the people shimmer.

The sun shines while you dine.
Swimming, skiing and playing
Whatever your heart desires.

As we see
The mountains and
The snowy slopes
The fog surrounds
Its mate
The Golden Gate.

It's home to
Mickey Mouse and
The Disney crew,
The Teen Pop
Sensation, The King
Of Pop and
The LA Lakers team.

Glamour is fashionable
On the streets
Of Beverly Hills
California, California, the
Place to be
Better than on your TV.

Priyanka Khanna (10)
Herington House School, Brentwood

My Dad's Car

My dad's car is like a beast
It is always raring to go.
It always has to have a big feast
Otherwise it will be slow.

It is like a cheetah
And drinks a litre.
It is very furious and fast
And never settles for coming last.

It is like a grizzly bear
But doesn't have any hair.
It is very, very scary
But not at all like a fairy.

It is just like an ape
Who likes eating grapes.
It is very big
And eats like a pig.

It is like a monkey,
Who is very funky.
When the music is playing
Everyone is saying,
'Hurrah, hurrah,
We love this car.'

Jack Salter (9)
Herington House School, Brentwood

The Monster In My Room

I went to my room one day
To have a little play.
When there I saw by the door,
A monster running away.

I looked around,
Upon the ground,
There was the monster again,
Actually on my toy train.

He turned it on,
And sat upon,
The carriage which was called Dom,
Unfortunately he ran away and then was gone.

My mum said,
'Tidy that room!'
I replied, 'But Mum, the monster,
Won't have anywhere at all to hide!'

Michael Percival (9)
Herington House School, Brentwood

The Sea

The sea is like a roller coaster
Rocking to and fro
Shaking, swaying, crashing down
I love to watch it go.

The wind has dropped, the sea is calm
A shiny, glistening hue,
It looks like a gleaming mirror,
In a beautiful sapphire-blue.

Adam Smith (10)
Herington House School, Brentwood

My Puppy

We have a puppy called Berrie,
She's small, furry and black.
I love our puppy Berrie,
Though she sometimes scratches my back!

Berrie is a Labrador dog,
Though Daddy sometimes calls her a rat.
She can be as jumpy as a frog,
And sometimes scares the cat!

When Berrie is quite sleepy,
She sniffs about my lap
Then she lies gently down,
And has a little nap!

When Berrie has woken up,
She runs and jumps about.
Then we open the back door,
And then she gallops out!

Mary Hirst (9)
Herington House School, Brentwood

Big Bill

There once was a man called Bill,
Who liked to eat his fill.
He ate too many pies,
With helpings of fries
And then Bill was feeling quite ill.

William Clarke (10)
Herington House School, Brentwood

My Duck, Milly

My duck is called Milly
She's as white as the snow
Her eyes are like sapphires
That glisten and glow.

She's beautiful and graceful
And swims so far.
That she could be in the Olympics
And become a star.

Head held high
She thinks she's a model
Her clumsy walk
Is more of a waddle.

Sometimes she's cheeky,
Sometimes she's not.
But either way
I'll still love her a lot.

Harriot Smith (10)
Herington House School, Brentwood

My Animals

First of all I'm going to talk about Sashabo,
She is my dog, she is so cute.
She plays in the sun, night and day
I love her so we love to play.

Second is my cat called Pop,
Poppsy Floppsy is so cute.
Every day she plays the flute
She dances round the living room.
I kiss her then she sleeps on a broom.

Thirdly there is my other cat,
Pip is the one who is big and fat.
Pipsy Wipsy is so cute,
She plays the drums and also the flute.
She sits on the sofa and sleeps all night,
She is my baby, I love her so with all my might.

Eden Hall (10)
Herington House School, Brentwood

Chocolate

Chocolate is tasty
Chocolate is yummy
Chocolate is better
When it's inside
My tummy.

Chocolate is dreamy
It's soft, dark and creamy.

What would I do if
Chocolate came to an end . . . ?

I can assure you it will
Be like losing a friend.

Brinkley Baglin (9)
Herington House School, Brentwood

My Sister

My sister Morgan is taller than me
And she lifts me up quite easily.
I can't lift her, I've tried and tried,
She must have something heavy inside!

Her shoes are big, her socks are long,
I run around for her all day long.
I fetch her drinks, I fetch her snacks,
Her favourites are those chocolate flapjacks.

She always annoys me and tells me what to do
I tried to get used to it, but what can I do?
So if you have a sister consider this please,
It's not always nice, it's hardly the bee's knees.

Kieran Wilson (9)
Herington House School, Brentwood

The Monster

Do monsters live in the cupboard?
Do monsters live under the bed?
Do monsters live in the cellar?
Or is it just all in my head?

Are monsters big, fat and hairy?
Are monsters disgustingly gross?
Are monsters squelchy and slimy?
Which monster would scare *you* the most?

My monster would have great big teeth,
My monster would eat sharks for tea,
My monster would growl like a grizzly bear,
My monster would belong to me.

Ethan Marshell (10)
Herington House School, Brentwood

Why?

Why do the stars twinkle at night?
Why does the sun shine so bright?
Why does the moon look so white?
Why does the dark sky give me a fright?

Why does the sea look so deep?
Lots of treasure, it must keep
Why do birds fly so high,
Way up high in the big blue sky.

Why does the grass grow so green?
Why do the leaves fall from the tree?
Why does the wind blow so cold?
Why do we all grow so old?

Daisy Oliphant (9)
Herington House School, Brentwood

Frost

Deep in the night frost comes calling,
Nobody's about to see it falling.
While everyone is sleeping sound,
It floats, gently to the ground.

It sits itself on the window ledge,
Till it melts and falls off the edge.
In the morning when we wake,
The frost is like a glistening lake.

It covers everything from grass to trees,
And chases away the birds and bees.
Then at last the sun comes out,
Melting the frost and bringing back colour all about.

Mahika Naidoo (10)
Herington House School, Brentwood

Months Of The Year

January is the start of the year,
February means spring is near,
March is when the daffodils bloom,
April brings the Easter moon,
May is when the birds start to sing,
June is when the wedding bells ring,
July is when school is out,
August means we are out and about,
September is when we are back to school,
October sees the leaves fall,
November is full of the firework crescents,
December is when you hope for presents.

Anna Moore (10)
Herington House School, Brentwood

The Dragon

I thought I was dreaming when before my eyes,
There came at me a great surprise.

Before me stood a massive dragon,
Drinking from a giant flagon.

The colour of his scales were types of red,
He made me shrink into my bed.

His mouth was full of flaring flames,
I don't think he fancied playing games.

He scowled and looked down at my way,
Then turned and ran far, far away.

Henry Linnell (9)
Herington House School, Brentwood

The Great Day - Haiku

I went to the beach
I got an ice cream; yummy
But then it went *splat!*

Bethany Little (10)
Ixworth Middle School, Ixworth

Horse!

I'm big,
But sometimes smaller.
I've got four legs,
I'm any colour.
I live in the wild,
Or inside.
I eat hay,
Every day!
I love being groomed,
Or even bathed.
I could be a bay
But might be a grey.
I'm tacked with a saddle,
And controlled with a bridle.
I love being ridden,
But best of all,
There's eating and sleeping!

Zosia Gryf-Lowczowska (10)
Kimbolton Preparatory School, Huntingdon

A Mouldy Pie

Flies buzzing
Fumes rising
Toxic flying
Help, anyone!
Life draining
Oxygen dying
Tummy churning
Disgust taking over
Repulse flooding
Death shooting.

Maddy Ando (9)
Kimbolton Preparatory School, Huntingdon

A Cup Of Tea

Cups at the ready, here it comes,
Under pressure to get a nice one,
Peppermint, Earl Grey or normal, which one?
Peppermint, hoorah, that's it done,
Steam starts coming out the spout,
The tea is ready to pour out,
Ahh, here it comes, oh boy,
Sipping it down, oh, the joy!

Isabelle Goodsall (10)
Kimbolton Preparatory School, Huntingdon

Lollipops

Lollipops
Luscious, appetising,
Licking, slurping, munching
Lemon, lime, strawberry, orange
Sucking, chomping, enjoying
Flavourful, sugary
Sweets.

Rowan Anderson (11)
Kimbolton Preparatory School, Huntingdon

Puppies

Puppies are playful, puppies are fun,
But my puppy is number one,
She has black furry hair and a pretty face,
But sometimes her fur grows so long, we have to tie it with a lace.
And even though my puppy is bold,
She is the best puppy in the world.

Shira Webb (8)
Kimbolton Preparatory School, Huntingdon

Midnight Avenue

The owl's hooting like an old bassoon,
The fox prowling as soft as an oboe,
Stepping on strings of a guitar,
The crow screeching like a recorder,
The mice scurrying like a maraca,
And all the animals are gone by morning sun . . .

William Day (10)
Kimbolton Preparatory School, Huntingdon

Walking In The Woods

W alking in the woods
O wls live in the woods
O wls sleep in the day
D ucks in the ponds
L iam saw leaves
A nimals making homes
N ests in the trees
D ay was cold
S quirrels jumping in the trees.

Liam Marshall (9)
Leighton Primary School, Peterborough

Woodland Walk

W oodpeckers
O wls hooting
O vergrown grass
D ucks swimming
L ake flowing
A nimals walking
N ewts jumping
D eer sleeping
S nakes slithering.

Charleen Large (10)
Leighton Primary School, Peterborough

The Woodland

I see a woodpecker making a sound.
I see a fox chasing a rabbit.
I see ducks swimming in the pond.
I see a fox digging beyond.

Courtney Blake (9)
Leighton Primary School, Peterborough

Tiger, Tiger

Tiger, tiger getting ready to spy,
Tiger, tiger, watching prey passing by,
Tiger, tiger, get ready for your meal,
Tiger, tiger get ready to kill,
Tiger, tiger have a peep,
Just before you go to sleep.

**Courtney Blake, Lucy Mason, Michael Reed (9),
Jehu Parrish & Andrew Holt (10)**
Leighton Primary School, Peterborough

The Class Poem

I see Nibbles waking up
I see Mrs Marsh doing mental maths
I see the class in circle time
I see the class going to the tunnel
I see Miss Weetman helping children.

Michael Reed (9)
Leighton Primary School, Peterborough

Robins

Robin
Red redbreast
Worms in beak
Little
Fly.

Marcus Hales (9)
Leighton Primary School, Peterborough

Ponds

Ducks swimming
Animals running
Ponds flowing
People walking
Lilies floating.

Shannon Walker (9)
Leighton Primary School, Peterborough

Rhyming Poem

I see a squirrel climbing a tree.
I see a bird chasing a bumblebee.
I see a rabbit eating a carrot.
I see a fox eating a rabbit.

Andrew Holt (10)
Leighton Primary School, Peterborough

All About Cats

Some cats are fat,
Some cats are skinny,
Some cats are big,
Some cats are mini.

They can be messy,
They can be lazy,
They can be neat,
They can be crazy.

But I love all cats,
No matter how they might be,
You might not like cats,
So we will just have to disagree,
You see.

Morag Cameron (9)
Mayfield Primary School, Cambridge

Chesterton Eagles
Under 9's Football Team

At Chesterton Eagles we're all friends
In forward, midfield and defence.

A tall blonde boy called Owen
Past his defence gets no one.

My friend in midfield is big Vin
He often helps us get a win.

A curly striker, name of Josh
One day will make a lot of dosh.

As long as we have my mate Max
The other side cannot relax.

Skilful football comes from Gus
He scores so many goals for us.

If we didn't have our James
In the goal we'd lose more games.

The longest kick has Jamie
And footwork like Fellaini.

Great crosses come from Thomas,
He always keeps his promise.

Our centre midfield Sammy
Has kicked a great big whammy.

If we didn't have Joe Brunning
The other team would still be running.

The smiley, kind Sebastian
In goal is our bastion.

Our brilliant coach is John
Before he joined we never won (true).

The match reports by Jake
Are the icing on the cake.

At Chesterton Eagles we're all friends
In forward, midfield and defence.

Gus Pepper (9)
Mayfield Primary School, Cambridge

If I Tried To Bake A Cake

If I tried to bake a cake, I wonder what thing I would make.
A bat, a hat, a catazat or maybe even me.
A football, a tennis ball, a rackipin, a thininin.
(Whatever they might be).
If I tried to bake a cake I wonder what type I would make.
A fruit cake maybe? No? Why?
Ah yes you are right, (too fruity) I think I have gone cazootey.
A chocolate cake, a banana cake, a cazata cake
A tomato waiting cake.
A dancer cake, an enhancer cake with flowers on the side.
If I tried to bake a cake I wonder how I would decorate.
Flowers, hours, Eiffel Towers, there really is a lot to pick.
Smiles, Jeremy Kyle's (I don't know who he is).
Girls, twirls, Minnie swirls, I think that I need a drink.
Snoopin' spies, lovely pies, cheaters and their silly lies
(Which never seem to work).
I don't think I will make a cake, at least until I learn to bake.

Leonie Garner (8)
Mayfield Primary School, Cambridge

Elements

Water, fire, earth and air
Elements are everywhere.
Sometimes good sometimes bad
Water to grow, and water to
But can cause flash floods.
Fire for warmth but can be terrible.
Buildings crash to the ground in flames
Earth to live on and to cultivate crops.
But earthquakes bring landslides burying houses.
Air to breathe, air to blow leaves from trees.
Hurricanes bringing death and disease.
Tornadoes twist and tornadoes turn,
All the while causing misery.
Water, fire, earth and air
Elements are everywhere.

Connor Nicol (8)
Mayfield Primary School, Cambridge

Rivers

Rivers are things that flow,
Sometimes they are very slow.

They can be in different shapes and sizes
Fish swim sometimes in disguises.
People go fishing then they end up wishing.

If you fall in don't get in a spin
Please have a coat with a float
So you can get back to your boat.
Seaweed on your boat, then you hope
It doesn't get into your moat.

Ducks quack, seagulls go back, kingfishers watching for their meals
They feed on a banana peel.

Emily Hancock (8)
Mayfield Primary School, Cambridge

The Spirit Of Nature - Haikus

High up in the tree
A squirrel's hole you will see
Inside lies hard nuts

In the cracking tree
An owl is looking for prey
He's spotted a mouse

Spiders spin their webs
To catch flies for their dinner
They drink the flies' blood

Snakes slither around
They are highly venomous
Snakes can eat large deer.

Owen Aldis (8)
Mayfield Primary School, Cambridge

This Is My Poem

This is my poem
Only my poem
This poem is about
Crunchy things!

Crunchy crisps
Crunchy caramel
Crunchy cheese
Crunchy crust
Crunchy cars
Crunchy cocktails
Crunchy and crisp . . .

Carrots!

Delia Diaz-Santana (8)
Mayfield Primary School, Cambridge

My Birthday Butterflies

They came in a pot full of stuff,
We wondered if there was enough.
They started to wiggle,
Some looked like a squiggle.
Fat and hairy, their skin was all rough.

They crawled to the top and began
Building cocoons in which they would hang.
We waited and waited
Until nature created
Pretty butterflies to which we all sang
Happy birthday to you
Painted ladies.

Gina Learmond (8)
Mayfield Primary School, Cambridge

Jedi Knights

J ustice keepers
E nergetic
D aredevils
I ntelligent

K ind
N ever stand down
I deal
G uardians of peace
H eroes
T rustworthy
S aviours of the galaxy.

Luke Carlson (8)
Mayfield Primary School, Cambridge

Winter

It is cloudy and gloomy,
No sunshine
The stars are sparkling
In the sky.
Very little day
But big nights
Christmas is nearly here
Santa is coming
To give some gifts
Watch out
If he is coming in!

Annesha Aboni Hassan (9)
Mayfield Primary School, Cambridge

Busy Bugs

Busy flies flying around.
Busy spiders swinging on their webs.
Busy bees getting nectar.
Busy slugs making tracks.

Now the rain comes
Bye-bye flies,
Bye-bye spiders,
Bye-bye bees,
Bye-bye slugs.

I hope you'll come back soon.

Max Anderson (9)
Mayfield Primary School, Cambridge

Swimming · Haikus

Oh I love swimming
Back stroke, side stroke, front stroke too
Swimming is such fun!

Oh I love swimming
Cutting through the shiny waves
Warm water splashes.

Oh I love swimming
Shiny waves hurdle sharp rocks
In I jump: *splash, splosh!*

Francesca Pellegrini (8)
Mayfield Primary School, Cambridge

Look At The . . .

Look at the sun that's boiling hot,
Tonnes of fire, jump on the spot.

Look at the river that flows into the sea.
It suddenly meets the power when it hits the sea.

Look at the forest with all the trees and bees
So fresh and vast it will bring you to your knees.

Look at the waterfall, the power and the shower.
It will take your heart away once you feel the glamour.

Amir-Reza Abbas-Hashemi (8)
Mayfield Primary School, Cambridge

The Shy Pony

I walked along the dark, dark street
And I didn't know what I would meet.

I heard footsteps *clip-clopping* in the night
And thought I saw something shining bright.

It had pink shaded fur and a long white mane
And eyes that were white with fright.

'Don't be scared!' I said to that pony
'Come with me and you won't be lonely!'

Etienne Chapelot (8)
Mayfield Primary School, Cambridge

Gently Down The River

Row, row, row your boat
Gently down the river
If you see another boat
Don't forget to steer

Row, row, row your boat
Gently down the river
If you see a waterfall
Don't forget to shiver.

Chanumi Gamage (8)
Mayfield Primary School, Cambridge

The River

The river is as beautiful as the sea.
The river is nice and sometimes very freezing.
The fish live in the river.
The river starts on the mountain then
It ends in the sea.
The Earth has lots of rivers.
The Amazon is one of the largest rivers in the whole world.
The river is really special to everyone.

Maria Cavalcanti (8)
Mayfield Primary School, Cambridge

The Snowman

The snow came to visit one day,
White and cold, on our garden it lay.
'What can we do with all this snow?' I said
My brother said, 'Build a snowman with a big head.'
We all started work on building the snowman,
Using a carrot for its nose and a stick for its hands.
Ice-cold was the snowman's head when you felt it,
I woke up early the next day, the snowman was gone, he had melted.

Nazir Ahmed (8)
Mayfield Primary School, Cambridge

Rivers · Haikus

Water continues
All the way into the sea
Then evaporates.

Ducks swim in rivers
And the fish also swim there
While the people watch.

Aaron Yuan (8)
Mayfield Primary School, Cambridge

My River

My name is Alistair
I live by the river
I like to cycle by it
I like to walk by it
I like the fish and ducks
But most of all I like eating
Ice creams by it.

Alistair Beynon (8)
Mayfield Primary School, Cambridge

I Love Food!

I love food.
I really like it.
I like cauliflower, I eat it everywhere.
I love sausages so I have seconds.
I eat leeks and if I don't have them I throw a tantrum
I really like to eat yummy marshmallows.
I like all of those but I hate carrots!

William Pearson (8)
Mayfield Primary School, Cambridge

Sunrise

S un coming out to play
U mbrellas shall be put away
N oisy birds singing all day
R eptiles and every other animal say hooray
I cicles and snow banished from the land
S o everyone shakes one another's hand
E veryone looking forward to the sun rising again.

Lottie Parslew (8)
Mayfield Primary School, Cambridge

Nature · Haikus

Down low in the grass
There lived a shivering mole
As he drilled away

See a white snow bird
In a stream of golden ray
Flying above sky.

Yu Ito (8)
Mayfield Primary School, Cambridge

Rivers

R ain falls
I t flows down the mountain
V alleys it has made
E ating away the riverbank
R ain starts it all
S earching for the sea.

Danny Evetts (8)
Mayfield Primary School, Cambridge

My Kittens

K ittens very playful, running here and there
I n and out of cupboards, climbing everywhere
T iny little noses, tiny little paws
T read very carefully, and slowly close the doors.
E agerly waiting for their mother to come in
N ow they are all feeding, you cannot hear a thing.

Daisy Reeve-Butler (8)
Mayfield Primary School, Cambridge

The Willow Tree

W illow trees are really wavy
I t waves and waves day to night
L ike a little rainbow flight
L ower each day the branches go
O h I've never seen that sight
W illow tree, goodnight!

Helin Topalca (8)
Mayfield Primary School, Cambridge

Rivers

Rivers look mysterious,
Rivers are full of life,
Rivers make me feel wonderful,
Rivers are calming,
When I stand by a river, I feel peaceful.
I like rivers.

Le-An Hoang (9)
Mayfield Primary School, Cambridge

Margot Littlefair

My friend Margot Littlefair,
Lucky is her cuddly bear.
Swimming is what we like to do,
Making funny pictures too.
We make each other feel better,
When we write each other letters.

Erica von Hippel (9)
Mayfield Primary School, Cambridge

The Three Bears

Once upon a time there were three bears
The father of the family was a nightmare.
Their house, it was not far from Norwich
They all loved to eat warm toasty porridge.

One day the porridge was too hot
They'd obviously turned up the oven a lot!
Off they went into the wood
To find a new oven if they could.
While they were out who appeared at the door?
Goldilocks clutching a pear core.

She kicked down the door and stepped inside
She slipped and fell and nearly cried.
She chose the chairs, first of all, so she sat on the big one
She saw the window and the bright yellow sun.

The little one was best - it was cute you see
It broke, she fell and hurt her knee.
She spied the porridge and ate it all up,
She spilt a lot - what a mucky pup!

Feeling tired she went up to bed
She got under the covers and laid down her head.
The bears returned and said, 'Oh my!'
The house it looked just like a pigsty.
'My chair, my porridge,' Baby said with a sob.
The chair repairer had got a new job.
'Let's check upstairs,' said Daddy Bear
And there was Goldilocks lying right there . . .

Lauren Scott (11)
Middleton (VC) Primary School, King's Lynn

Rain

The rain trickling down the window
Is a spider
Hanging on a single thread,
Going up and down
Spinning a silky web.

The rain trickling down the window
Is a bird
Flying gracefully in the sky,
Calling for thousands more to come.

The rain trickling down the window,
Is a leaf
Floating down from a big tree.

It's the crackling sound
As if leaves are being walked on.

Shannon Hill (11)
Middleton (VC) Primary School, King's Lynn

White Linen

The remains of an unwanted ghost,
A fallen ceiling,
A puffy cloud, floating in the sky,
The pale features of the waves.

The wings of an eagle,
The mane of a unicorn,
The breath of a whale,
The flippers of a penguin.

The unspoken word,
A lifeless shroud,
The frosty ice,
The end of a soul . . .

Edward Little (11)
Middleton (VC) Primary School, King's Lynn

The Weather

The sun burning everyone
Is a fierce lion, prince of the country
Roaring and screaming
Engulfing the world!

The snow floating around the village
Is a polar bear, king of the ice
Roaring and scratching
Engulfing the sea!

The fog passing through the air
Is a cat, queen of the village
Purring and clawing
Engulfing the country!

Hannah Footer (10)
Middleton (VC) Primary School, King's Lynn

Postcard Poem

A t Alton Towers I
L oved it, we went on the
T errific spinball whizzer. It broke down
O n us so we got to go on it straight away again.
   We went on it
N ine

T imes. We also went
O n the squirrel nutty ride for my brother Leon.
W e were drenched because it
E ventually
R ained. All in all we had a
S uperb time.

Bradley Allen (10)
Middleton (VC) Primary School, King's Lynn

Dawn Of The Dead

I am Age
I have nothing left of me
My face has no features, just mould
My body is like a skeleton
Not much flesh, only bones
My feet are stone-cold with only my big toe
I am ageing to dust
Ageing . . .
Ageing . . .
Ageing . . .
Dust.

James Meaney (11)
Middleton (VC) Primary School, King's Lynn

Weather

The lightning flashing around at midnight
Is a cheetah fast
Pouncing and leaping on its prey!

The tornado spinning and taking up the strongest of trees
Is a monkey
Scratching and pouncing on its prey!

The snowflake gentle as it touches the cold ground
Is a polar bear
Camouflaged and flaking to
Nothing!

Tyler Carey (10)
Middleton (VC) Primary School, King's Lynn

Arctic Garden

The snow,
Is a penguin,
Drifting on my garden,
Squawking and waddling,
Down to the fish-infested pond.

The ice,
Is an Arctic fox,
Blanketing my flower garden,
Padding and stalking,
On the unsuspecting.

Alastair Legg (10)
Middleton (VC) Primary School, King's Lynn

Anger!

I am Anger!
I have a red face and
A boiling hot body,
My eyes are bloodshot
I am bursting with rage
As I roar with anger!
As I shout!
As I scream!
Bursting
Like a volcano!

Jessie Davies (11)
Middleton (VC) Primary School, King's Lynn

Death

I am Death
I am a devil
Raging with
Anger.
I am a black shadow
Emerging
From the darkness
Like a bull charging towards me
With razor-sharp horns.
I am *Death!*

Josh Johns (11)
Middleton (VC) Primary School, King's Lynn

A Dead Man's Shroud

The shroud is the flowing sea,
The frothy waves curling over each other.

A dolphin jumping through the sea,
The tail of a unicorn galloping through the air
Then floating through the air like a feather.

A fluffy cloud travelling through the air,
Softly floating on the wind,
Absorbing water then letting it go
Splish, splash, splosh.

Harrison Sturgess (11)
Middleton (VC) Primary School, King's Lynn

Happiness!

I am Happiness!
Whirling and twirling
On a summer's day
Skipping round the beach
As my ice cream drips down my hand

I jump into the sea,
Catching every wave possible,
As it knocks my knees
Booming and *crashing!*

Tilly Fisher (10)
Middleton (VC) Primary School, King's Lynn

Disease

I am Disease,
I have rotten, wrinkled skin,
Heavy bloodshot eyes,
I'm a frenzied shiver,
My thoughts are dead,
My soul is
Bleeding,
Fading
Drying up!

Ben Dobbing (11)
Middleton (VC) Primary School, King's Lynn

Pain!

I am Pain.
I have blood pouring from my scratched up body
I have bloodshot eyes that water
My hands are like torn up rags
I screech out in pain and agony
It's like my soul is bleeding
Bleeding
Dying
Dead.

Cameron Wright (10)
Middleton (VC) Primary School, King's Lynn

Weather

The storm crashing down
Is a tiger leaping on its prey
Roaring and stalking
Crushing down anything in its path!

The fog crawling around my house
Is a hamster, the master of stealth
Prancing and racing
Surrounding the Earth!

Finn Carey (10)
Middleton (VC) Primary School, King's Lynn

Rain

The rain crashing on my house
Is an angry leopard,
Crushing the roof tiles
Making me wet
And flooding my house.

Jack Walker (11)
Middleton (VC) Primary School, King's Lynn

Death

I am Death!
I wear a dark
Cloak of rotten skulls,
I take people
And crush them to bits!
I tear them apart and smash them
I am the Devil of *Death!*

Daniel Barr (11)
Middleton (VC) Primary School, King's Lynn

The Rain

The rain is like
A lion crushing my home.
The rain is like
A gorilla chucking bananas.
The rain is like
A jaguar
Speeding through my house.

Luke Gooding (10)
Middleton (VC) Primary School, King's Lynn

Holiday Postcard

B illy Bear was great
U bot the robot was awesome
T ime went fast
L ittle Imogen feeding the ducks
I t all stopped
N othing is better than Butlins
S till it was fun!

Zac King (11)
Middleton (VC) Primary School, King's Lynn

Anger

I am Anger
My eyes are fire
I am black inside
My legs are kicking out
My hands are curled up
My whole body is like steel.

Archie Holman (11)
Middleton (VC) Primary School, King's Lynn

Snow

The snow gently laying on the ground
Like a pillow of wool
A puppy, gently rolling about into it
Enjoying and playing
In the snow!

Ryan Wilson (11)
Middleton (VC) Primary School, King's Lynn

If I Had A Dog

If I had a dog
I would play with her all day long
Run around and have races
Until we were too tired.

We would go swimming in the sea
Swimming around
Just her and me
Until we were freezing cold

Lying on the ground under the blazing hot sun
Rolling around in the dirty wet mud
Until we got very muddy.

Shannon Bird (9)
Mill Vale School, Dunstable

Snow

Crispy snow beneath my feet,
Drifting around snow and sleet.
As it falls to the ground,
It spreads like butter on toast.

As I walk forward
My footprints left behind
In the thick, silky snow
So as I walk forward people see what way I go.

The great icy mountain,
Looks like a huge pile of sugar.
Going up higher and higher
The cottony snow view was my desire.

Sledging down
Faster I go
Whizzing around
Melting the snow.

At home my clothes put by the fire
Looking out the window I see
A car skidding on its tyre
10 o'clock
Having creamy cocoa chocolate.
As it touches my lip
It drizzles into my cold, empty stomach.

Alex Catlin (9)
Mill Vale School, Dunstable

If I Had A Plane
(Inspired by 'If I had Wings' by Pie Corbett)

If I had a plane
I would fly anywhere
I wanted to and have
An exciting adventure.

If I had a plane
I would fly over the
White cotton clouds.

If I had a plane
I would fly close
To the bright blue sea.

If I had a plane
I would fly to many cities
And meet new people.

If I had a plane
I would take my friends
For a ride.

If I had a plane
I would fly over the bright,
Light cities below.

Bradley Taylor (10)
Mill Vale School, Dunstable

Daylight

Can be seen, cannot be smelt
Cannot be heard, cannot be felt.
Can be useful
If you're quite dim
Fills up gaps, helps with sight
You've got to be bright to work this out.

Ross Cooper (9)
Mill Vale School, Dunstable

Snow

White, soft, silky snow
But sometimes it has to go
People make snowmen and snowballs
And it can fall off snowy walls
Weather gets cold, so it snows everywhere.

Slippery, silver, dangerous ice
It is not very nice
Ice is as bad as an ice lolly
Ice, ice everywhere
So beware, for the devil ice.

Snowmen, snowflakes, sledging and igloos
People make snowmen with their big gloves
Snowflakes fall from the sky
Sledging, sledging, kids go sledging!
Igloos are fun and you can sleep in one.

Snow, snow, glorious snow!
Kids go out and play in it
Sometimes you slip
Sometimes you fall
So be careful in the silky snow.

Hannah Emerson (10)
Mill Vale School, Dunstable

Snowman

S tand in the snow
N ow let's make a snowman
O ver everything
W ow! Look at that snowman
M any people love the snow
A nyone can play
N ow it's time to go home, hip hip hooray.

Lucy Booth (10)
Mill Vale School, Dunstable

If I Had Gills

(Inspired by 'If I had Wings' by Pie Corbett)

If I had gills
What would I do?
I'd scour the ocean,
That deep, velvety blue.

If I had gills
I'd search for SpongeBob
And stand by his side
While he wrecked Plankton's plans.

If I had gills
I would swish like a mermaid
Swaying my exotic, rainbow tail
Tossing my golden locks
Dancing with my friends.

If I had gills
I'd leap like a dolphin
I'd skim like a Mantaray
I'd gallop like a sea horse
And be as sneaky as an eel
Oh if only I had gills . . .

Imogen Gurney (9)
Mill Vale School, Dunstable

School

Books, books, books
That's what we use all day.

Pens, pencils, paints
They're utensils we use every day
The teachers say be careful
Those books will tear.

My friend gets all upset
When she fails the test.
I say, 'Do not worry
You'll do better next time.'

When it's the end of the day
I don't want to leave
Because it's so much fun
My friends all throw a party,
Because the day is through,
But I don't like it because it makes me feel alone.

When I get home I do my homework,
The thing I don't like is I am not allowed to watch TV
Until the deed is done.

Jenna Louise Sage (9)
Mill Vale School, Dunstable

My Annoying Brother

I have a very annoying brother
Who likes to play and shout very loud
He likes to eat in his sleep
That's my brother in the night.

In the day he's very energetic
He likes to play on our swing
He plays and plays until he feels sick.

Harry Springer (10)
Mill Vale School, Dunstable

If I Were A Dog
(Inspired by 'If I had Wings' by Pie Corbett)

If I were a dog
I would chase my tail
Around and around
In a garden.

If I were a dog
I would run faster
Than a car
When I went for long walks.

If I were a dog
I would lick myself
Clean when I got dirty.

If I were a dog
I would eat cold,
Canned food.

If I were a dog
I would eat
My chewy bone
Until it was gone.

Danielle Barden (10)
Mill Vale School, Dunstable

What Am I?

Running jumper
Tail wagger
Speedy runner
Cat chaser
Meat lover
People kisser.

I am a dog.

Elize Burke-Radcliffe (9)
Mill Vale School, Dunstable

If I Had Two Pairs Of Hands
(Inspired by 'If I had Wings' by Pie Corbett)

If I had two pairs of hands
I would be able
To hold my baby sister,
Watch EastEnders
And finish my homework
At the same time.

If I had two pairs of hands
I would be able
To go on Facebook,
And play lots of games.

If I had two pairs of hands
I would be able to cook
And eat my dinner
And feed my sister.

If I had two pairs of hands
I would do gymnastics,
Sing on karaoke
And go jogging.

Gracie Dearne (10)
Mill Vale School, Dunstable

Football All The Way

Every time I get the ball
I always try to score.
When it's with the other team
I aim to tackle them.
If I score a screamer
And my dad is really pleased,
I always get congratulated
By the other team.

If I'm a goalkeeper
I'd do my very best,
I'd stop the opposition
From making it a draw.

If I was on the wing
I'd put them to sleep,
Of course I'd try and do my job,
I'd cross it into the box,
And then my other friends,
Would hopefully score in the goal.

And then we'd win the game!

Charlie McEvoy (10)
Mill Vale School, Dunstable

Snow

Snow is fun
But not to some
And most people play
In it all day.

The snow blizzards can be bad,
And that makes drivers quite mad.
Trains stop,
Plants flop.

School is shut,
Parents tut.
Children throw snowballs
As the white snow falls.

Winter is the best time for snow
It's nature's own special show.
Birds searching for their meal,
The crumbs on our window sill.

Snow is now melting away
Hopefully it will return another day.

Emily Surridge (9)
Mill Vale School, Dunstable

Fish

Fish swimming in the sea
Being free, as free as can be
Happily swishing their tails
Looking at people with their sails.

Happily gliding round and round
Looking to see what can be found
Shipwrecks sunken to the bottom of the sea
Thinking of what fish there could be.

Eleanor King (9)
Mill Vale School, Dunstable

Parents

Parents can be moody at times
Also very grumpy,
And if I am very naughty
They get in a mood.

But the worst thing is
When they shout loudly at me.
It makes me feel bad inside
But I soon get over it.

But even though they shout at me
I still love them very much,
And I wouldn't say I didn't
'Cause I do.

And the best thing about my parents
Is that they give me lots of love,
I never want to lose them
'Cause my parents are the
Best!

Olivia Braylin (9)
Mill Vale School, Dunstable

What Am I?

Cute cuddler
Carrot eater
Nice greeter
High hopper
Stringy whisker
Quick runner
Clever creeper
Black, white

I am a rabbit.

Fawn Barnett (10)
Mill Vale School, Dunstable

Tiger's Taken Away

The animal who's a feline
In a dark, dark cage
Left her cubs at home
And was very ashamed.

The blind cubs crying for their mother
To give them food of deer or a wild boar
Left to lay in the cold
And see her no more.

The mother waiting to pounce
To the keeper of her
To leave her alone
And to get her out.

The cubs growing up
Looking for a mate
Having a cub of their own
And never do what their mother
Did to them.

Ellie Whybrow (10)
Mill Vale School, Dunstable

Can You Guess What I Am?

Really fast
Very creepy
Body ripper
Sharp teeth
Blood slurper
Jaw snapper
Bone cruncher
Fish muncher

I'm a shark!

Megan White (10)
Mill Vale School, Dunstable

Football, Football

If I had the spotty ball,
I would shoot it in the big net!
Just as good,
As a superstar, just like Ronaldo.

If I was in goal,
I would try to play my best
Even if I let a goal in the big net,
But I would never give up!

If I had an injury,
I would not burst into lots of tears!
But I would get on my small feet,
And support . . . my dream team.

If I had the spotty ball
I would look at one
Of my best players
I would look up and down
To see if they were in space.

Christian Sorrentino (10)
Mill Vale School, Dunstable

What Am I?

Fast runner
Hay eater
Loud squeaker
Lazy sleeper
Good swimmer
Apple muncher
Weed cruncher
High jumper
I am a guinea pig.

Chloe McIntyre (9)
Mill Vale School, Dunstable

Pets

If I could choose a pet
It would probably be a horse
Galloping through the field
Eating fresh green grass.

If I had a horse
It would be a mare
I would want a brown horse
I would call her Pearl.

I would love her very much
I hope she would love me too
I would take care of her
Take her for rides every day.

At night
I would give her lots of straw
I would give her a carrot
If she got hungry,
And then tuck her in.

Megan Camfield (9)
Mill Vale School, Dunstable

Snow

Snow fast, snow slow
Snow everywhere around the globe
Snow up, snow down,
Gosh! Snowing makes me frown.

Slippery roads, slippery cars, slippery bikes
Slippery everything, *yikes!*
Freezing day, freezing sights,
How to get through icy nights.

People making snowmen white,
Children have snowball fights
Skiing, sledging, having fun
They're even doing it at night.

Days and nights of snow are fun
But I'd rather have the sun
I had a good time in the snow
But I have to let it go.

Mohammed Rizvi (10)
Mill Vale School, Dunstable

My Baby Brother

He's a
Night sleeper
Morning weeper
Chocolate stealer
Food muncher
Biscuit cruncher
Sweet scoffer
Dog lover
Cat chaser
Cheeky monkey
Louis lover.

Louis Giles (10)
Mill Vale School, Dunstable

My School!

Our ICT teacher is so cool
He loves to come and visit our school
When it comes to learning
He knows it all!

Our English teacher, she's the best
Far better than all the rest,
Always cold, she wears a vest,
She likes to watch birds in their nest!

Our art teacher, Mrs White
Really knows how to write
But her brillant paintings
Have caused many faintings!

Mrs Ellyard, she's so tough
When it comes to lessons
She knows her stuff
Well that's my head teacher, that's how she is!

Holly Stokes (10)
Mill Vale School, Dunstable

My Dog

Tail wagger
Slipper chewer
Ball chaser
Stick catcher
Hole digger
Sofa chewer
Attention seeker
Feet chewer
Toe licker
Food stealer
River swimmer.

Siân Exon (9)
Mill Vale School, Dunstable

Rabbits

Hoppity hop go the little bunnies
Hopping to and fro,
Racing through the wild flowers
Look at them go!

Soft, fluffy tails bobbing up and down,
All having fun,
Twisting, turning, jumping high,
In the winter sun.

Little bunny footprints printed in the snow,
Searching for a bite to eat,
Looking for their warm, cosy burrows,
To take their tasty treats.

At last they settle down to sleep,
After an active day,
Lots of exciting adventures,
The bunnies have had today!

Abbie Lampard (9)
Mill Vale School, Dunstable

Snow

It's soft and lumpy
For sledging it's bumpy
It turns to ice
For kids, it's nice.

It's white, it's cold
You can make a snowman
It's fluffy and fresh
It's not good for adults.
But it's good for kids.

Just simple snow

Kyra Imlach (9)
Mill Vale School, Dunstable

School

I have a really brill school
I wish it had a swimming pool
If I don't pay any attention
I will get a lot of detentions.

Maths, English, science
I love them all
Our science teacher
Is really cool!

Our English teacher
She knows it all
When it comes to punctuation
We have to underline it all.

Our maths teacher
The brainy one
When it comes to sums
She's the number 1!

Ellen Harrington (10)
Mill Vale School, Dunstable

What Am I?

Fast runner
Canine chewer
Teeth dipper
Powerful predator
Ferocious killer
Animal hunter
Meat liker
Fast killer
Speed demon.

I'm a tiger.

Ruhen Uddin (9)
Mill Vale School, Dunstable

My Family

I love my family
And I think they love me
They take me on trips
But not around the world.
There's my mum, my dad
And my sisters too.
There's my brother, my sister's boyfriend,
And my nephew.
I really love them
I do, I do.

They give me presents
And I say thank you
They play, they cook dinner
And they make me happy.
I say I love them
Because I do, I do.

Caitlin Planson (10)
Mill Vale School, Dunstable

If I Had An Elephant
(Inspired by 'If I had Wings' by Pie Corbett)

If I had an elephant,
I would take him everywhere,
And look after him forever.

If I had an elephant
I would travel with him
To exotic deserts and lay in the sun.

If I had an elephant
I would take him on an
Exciting adventure to the amazing
Amazon rainforest.

Alisha Lad (9)
Mill Vale School, Dunstable

And She Was Gone . . .

She didn't have companions or any enemies,
But she had something following her
And she tried to get rid of it
By climbing up some trees.

Some strings were attached to her
And she really got fed up,
She couldn't eat, run or jump
And she couldn't pour a cup.

Then she went to a mountain
Where there was a magic fountain
Let go of everything she had and she was gone
If you ever see her,
Don't touch her,
Or you will be a mystery
And you will be history.

Benita Mubiru-Lwanga (9)
Mill Vale School, Dunstable

Clocks

Clocks go tick-tock
Every single second
Pendulum swinging back and forth
Waiting for the hour
When it strikes at 12 o'clock
It is as loud as a lion's roar.

People staring at the clock
Waiting for the news
'Time for break,' the teacher says
The children shout, 'Yippee!'
Next time you look at the clock
Remember the time you read this poem.

Georgia Mulholland (10)
Mill Vale School, Dunstable

If I Had Fins
(Inspired by 'If I had Wings' by Pie Corbett)

If I had fins
I would swim the deep
Blue sea
And swim with the lively dolphins.

If I had fins
I would see the colourful
Coral reef.
And play with the
Happy fish.

If I had fins
I would find the
Gigantic Titanic
And find the golden treasure
That lurks below.

Callum Mackie (10)
Mill Vale School, Dunstable

My Bunny

Hip hopper
Carrot cruncher
Lettuce muncher
Sloppy drinker
Jumps higher
Hard scratcher
Toy hider
Toy finder
Tail fluffer
Bed curler
Flip flopper
Mean nipper.

Elisha Patel (9)
Mill Vale School, Dunstable

My Cat

I have a very furry cat,
She likes to play a lot of games,
She sits upon my lap
Falling asleep
She can dream away all night.
But when she wakes up again,
She needs feeding.
Like she does at lunch and evening.
My cat is as furry as a lion's mane
She is the laziest cat I know
She is a female
And a tortoiseshell cat.
That's my cat for you
She is very important to me!

Miaow!

Louise Sturdee (9)
Mill Vale School, Dunstable

The Zoo

One day I went to the zoo
I saw a kangaroo
He jumped up in the sky,
It seemed like he could fly.

Further down on the way
I saw some penguins play
They loved to do hockey
One of them was even a jockey.

I kept on walking down the path,
The next thing I saw was a hippo in a bath.
Scrubbing, scrubbing, trying to get clean,
I looked at him again and it made him gleam.

Chloe Hunter (9)
Mill Vale School, Dunstable

If I Had A Rabbit

(Inspired by 'If I had Wings' by Pie Corbett)

If I had a rabbit
It would be my best friend.

If I had a rabbit
I would play with it all the time
And teach it to do tricks.

If I had a rabbit
I would comb its fur
Until it shone like the stars at night
And then play with it again.

If I had a rabbit
It would follow me around
Until the sun goes down behind the hills,
And then we would go to sleep until the next day.

Faye Giddings (9)
Mill Vale School, Dunstable

My Brother

He's a
Biscuit stealer
Coke drinker
Broccoli hater
Finger licker
Bubble blower
Messy monster
Dog feeder
Cat disliker
Football fanatic
Computer breaker
Ben destroyer
Telly owner.

Ben Brown (10)
Mill Vale School, Dunstable

If I Had Fins
(Inspired by 'If I had Wings' by Pie Corbett)

If I had fins
I would dive to the bottom
Of the sea and collect
All of the golden treasure.

If I had fins
I would swim with the
Scaly tailed mermaids
And play with the
Multicoloured fish.

If I had fins
I would battle the
Sharks with help from
The sneaky dolphins.

Charlotte Camfield (9)
Mill Vale School, Dunstable

Take A Second Look

At the back of every igloo
In the middle of the room
You might come across me
As you eat through your food
You will always see me doing
Loop-the-loop
When you order ice cream
You might say two scoops
To work out this riddle
It might be a fiddle
But all you really have to do
Is to look into the
Middle of the moon.

Sam Neale (9)
Mill Vale School, Dunstable

Families!

I love my family
And they love me.
If they were to disappear,
I don't know what I'd do.
I have family all over the world!
Germany, England, America.
But sometimes I wish we were all together,
All in one country, all happy, together,
Forever.

I have two cousins in America.
I have a dad in Germany.
I have a mum and crazy brother in England.
But like I said, I wish we were all happy,
All together forever.

Jennifer Senft (10)
Mill Vale School, Dunstable

The Penguin

Penguin thinking of the snow,
The snow that used to be its home.

Dreaming of the slippery ice
He remembers, it used to be sooo nice!

But nice isn't a word to describe it,
This hurts him inside and he doesn't like it.

The other penguins he doesn't know
It seems to him the day goes so slow!

I'm not saying animals in captivity is bad,
But just remember, it makes them very sad!

Phoebe Edwards (10)
Mill Vale School, Dunstable

My Sister's Orang-utan

On Christmas Day a big surprise
Awaits under the Christmas tree for my sister's eyes
In a colourful box awaits an orang-utan so sweet.
It starts to cry and gently weeps.
With its big bulging eyes and its big brown belly,
It jumps onto the sofa and starts to watch telly.
When all of a sudden it hears a big sound
Of pattering feet quick on the ground.
As the door opens wide she gets a big shock,
As two children came down wearing bed socks.
My sister is happy with what she can see.
A baby orang-utan that now is happy.
Just what she wanted, the very one thing
The best Christmas present that Santa could bring.

Emily Hogg (9)
Mill Vale School, Dunstable

Snow

Snow falling down and down,
Time to put on my dressing gown.

School shut, hip hip hooray
Time to see the winter parade.

Me and my friends have been sledging all day
Come home hungry from our long play.

Come home, put my clothes by the fire,
Then I see the ice melting with desire

Get into bed, bump my head,
Another day gone, while I eat a scone.

Matthew Griggs (9)
Mill Vale School, Dunstable

What Am I?

Food stealer
Speedy runner
Belly rubber
Funny sleeper
Tail chaser
Slimy liker
Biscuit eater
Loud barker
Silent barker
Crazy eater.

I am a dog.

Lewis Gobey (10)
Mill Vale School, Dunstable

What Am I?

Stick leaver
Good hider
Egg leaver
Cool camouflager
Good bouncer
Wall climber
Fast hopper
Violent silencer
Good daydreamer
Good sleeper.

I am a frog.

Abigail Cowley (10)
Mill Vale School, Dunstable

What Am I?

Cat chaser
Mouse killer
Fast swimmer
Mad jumper
Crazy player
Crazy runner
Meat lover
Tail chaser
Barking mad
Speedy runner.

I am a dog.

Bradley Miller (10)
Mill Vale School, Dunstable

What Am I?

Milk licker
Water hater
Vicious tracker
Kid hater
Loud muncher
Furry monster
Feet flapper
Powerful catcher
Fierce biter
Claw scraper.

I am a cat.

Zoe Jetke (10)
Mill Vale School, Dunstable

What Am I?

Speedy chaser
Meat ripper
Dawn hunter
Paw licker
Bone cruncher
Big muncher
Claw scraper
Meat eater
Grass creeper
Lazy sleeper.

I am a cheetah.

James Parker-Harvey (9)
Mill Vale School, Dunstable

What Am I?

Loud barker
Bone cruncher
Meat eater
Tail chaser
Fast runner
Cat chaser
Good jumper
Fierce fighter
Good swimmer
Fur biter.

I am a dog.

Brandon Prince (9)
Mill Vale School, Dunstable

What Am I?

Meat eater,
Dawn hunter,
Paw licker
Grass creeper,
Lazy sleeper,
Super climber
Cub killer,
Claw scraper,
High leaper,
Huge muncher.

I am a tiger.

Alex Carr (10)
Mill Vale School, Dunstable

What Am I?

Man killer
Fast swimmer
Lanky grower
Slimy crawler
Toxic biter
Human frightener
Meat lover
Blood stealer
Body stealer
Slow predator.

I am a python.

Ben McGregor (9)
Mill Vale School, Dunstable

What Am I?

Speedy runner
Scatter sleeper
Silent wheeler
Big cruncher
Sweet teether
Super climber
Fruit eater
Water kisser
Eye blinker
Fur washer

I'm a hamster!

Sam Bowley (10)
Mill Vale School, Dunstable

What Am I?

Loud barker
Cat chaser
Mad jumper
Crazy player
Mouse killer
Fast runner
Crazy boxer
Meat lover
Tail chaser
Crazy barker.

I am a dog.

Lewis Pike (9)
Mill Vale School, Dunstable

Football, Football, Football

All the players in their positions
Being cheered on by all their fans
All you can see is their waving hands.
Football, football, football.

They shoot a goal, everyone roars
Half-time here, everyone rushes
For a pint of beer.
Football, football, football.

The referee blows his whistle
Half-time's ended.
Hopefully the defender will defend it.
Football, football, football.

Another team scores
Only seconds left
Who will win?
Football, football, football.

Brinley Crick (7)
Moorlands CE Primary School, Great Yarmouth

Poetry Express

The dog was friends with a frog
My dad was mad about the cat
My dog kept playing with a frog
The cat sat on the mat with a rat
The rat kept playing with the cat
The mouse had a very large house
The rat had a teddy cat
The bee had a large knee.

Destiny Dorrington (8)
Moorlands CE Primary School, Great Yarmouth

Snow

The snow was shimmering all around,
Just like a penny falling to the ground.
You don't hear snow with a bang or a thud,
You just see it fluttering to the mud.

I put on my gloves, scarf and hat,
And I thought to myself, *I want to play in that!*
So I went outside and it was freezing cold,
The sun was out and the snow twinkled gold.

The trees were swaying in the breeze,
Just like my knobbly knees.
I decided to go home
Before I ended up just like a gnome.

Victoria Blake (8)
Moorlands CE Primary School, Great Yarmouth

I Like Cars

I like cars
I like cars that are fast.
I like cars that fly through the air
I like cars that look good.
I like cars with a big engine.
I like cars that are racing.
I like cars.

Harry Lance Raven (8)
Moorlands CE Primary School, Great Yarmouth

My Mum

I love my mum with all my heart
I miss her when we are apart.
She makes me lots of chocolate brownies,
Which are my favourite treats,
They are very yummy and taste very sweet.

Maisie Kerrison (7)
Moorlands CE Primary School, Great Yarmouth

My Dog

I have a dog and her name is Poppy,
I have a dog and we walk her four times a day,
I have a dog and she is very lovely,
I have a dog and I love her very much,
I have a dog and we picked the most lovely dog ever.

Megan Jade Webb (8)
Moorlands CE Primary School, Great Yarmouth

Snow

Snow, snow, snow, snow
Raindrops falling
The sun coming out
The world melting
I can see outside.

I think my friend will die
Please sun, don't kill my snowman
I love the snow
Snowflakes in my mouth.

People crying,
'I love the snow'
Me as well for sure.

Noreen Sultan (10)
Moorlands School, Luton

If I Were A Mountaineer

If I were a mountaineer
I'd climb the mountains high
I'd leap and jump to the top
To watch the clouds go by.

The mountains are my friend and foe
Happiness and treachery as I go
Blizzards, avalanches or just slippery slopes
Oh how I have to watch as I go.

Mountains big or mountains small,
One little trip and you could fall,
Breaking bones and crushing ribs
Or the bleak joys of being on the missing list.

Small or big, bleak and bland
Is it snow or is it land?
Crashing down, down below
Would you survive?
I don't know.

Making sure you wear the gear
Not for Sloane Square
But for being a mountaineer
Waterproofs and big warm socks
Oh and I nearly forgot
Take some food in case you get lost
On your adventures to the top.

Arabella Cadore (10)
Moorlands School, Luton

Journey Into Space

Countdown,
5, 4, 3, 2, 1,
The rocket rumbles,
A loud explosion,
Lift off,
Up, up and away we go,
We pass the sun,
We pass the stars,
We enter the dark unknown.
What planet could this be?
Is it Jupiter, Mars, Pluto or Neptune?
No it's the moon,
We get out, we explore,
Oh we're floating,
I can see footprints,
Could there be aliens?
Could there be life on the moon?
Oh no, it's Neil Armstrong,
It's time to come back to Earth now,
Oh no, we've run out of fuel!
Houston, we have a problem!

Sana Zaman (8)
Moorlands School, Luton

School Is So Cool

School is so cool
So I play football
Tennis is fun
And I eat buns for lunch
Don't hit me because
I will karate chop your head off
History is so, so me at school.

James Turner (8)
Moorlands School, Luton

Travel Through Space!

Zooming through outer space
A beam falls on us,
Red, purple, yellow, blue,
Then everything goes blank . . .
Aliens of red and blue,
Advance on our rocket ship!

They ruin all the metalwork
And turn it green!
They break all the glass
And turn it all black!
What a day, what a day,
Day with the UFOs!

What a weird and wonderful experience
On the North Pole planet: spots!
But there's nothing as weird and wonderful,
As a journey through outer space!

Helena Milton (8)
Moorlands School, Luton

King Beast

Ambushing carnosaurus
Heavyweight killer
King lizard
Loud roarer
Slow runner
Powerful beast
Mad meat-eater
Bone crusher
Power eater
Maximum power
Menacing meat-eater.

Vaishnav Shinde (7)
Moorlands School, Luton

UF Uh-Oh!

I was travelling in space,
And all of a sudden,
I wanted to race!
I looked around,
There was no one,
And then I saw a ship,
It was quite round!

It flew so low
That I couldn't see it
And then I knew it was a Uf Uh-Oh!
I flew as fast as I could,
But the *UFO was gaining on me!*
But I crashed in a piece of wood!

The UFO helped me
And said, 'Did you want to race?'
I said, 'No, not now, I really have to pee!'

Aksh Tailor (9)
Moorlands School, Luton

Travelling In Space

I'm travelling in space, wow! Look at it and look at that
Red planet Mars, its colour matches my underpants.
Wow, and half the moon looks like cheese!

Oh no! A big moon rock is about to fall on me!
Now I'm travelling through space about to get squashed
Like ants . . . Finally it's gone . . .

Oh no! A UFO is after me, it's red like lava and huge like
Four grown elephants, and it's shooting like mad . . .
Finally it's gone . . . Now I'm out of petrol . . .
Uh oh, here comes the rock!

Hasan Ahmed (8)
Moorlands School, Luton

The Sea Adventure

Hoist the sail! Steer for the sea,
Wave goodbye to the shore happily,
We're on a yacht, on a fine sunny day!

A cry for help, 'Man overboard'
Terrified cries, 'Shark! Shark!'
Swim for the boat as fast as you can.

Throw out the sandwiches,
Keep shark away,
Clutch onto the lifeboat, up and away.

Back on ship, safe and sound,
Thank you, skilled doctor
I'm back on safe ground.

Back to land with a strong gust of wind,
Moor the yacht, we're home again.
Next time we will take the train!

Katie Lachlan (8)
Moorlands School, Luton

Apes

Banana eater
Flea picker
Vine swinger
Tree climber
Tree liver
Very loud
Furry coated
Rubbery skin
Apple eaters
Funny chaps.

Cheryl Mangoro (7)
Moorlands School, Luton

Little Brother

Very annoying
In the family
Trouble maker
Not tidy
Younger person
Wants everything
Small boy
TV stealer
Stress maker
Very cheeky
Bad loser
Show off
Born after.

Alana Pillai (8)
Moorlands School, Luton

My Teacher - Mrs Murray

Today my teacher is feeling . . .

Happy as a hippo
Cold as a cream cake out of the fridge
Crazy as a kangaroo
Blonde as a balloon
Pretty as a penny
Worried about her hair
Carrying her hairbrush
Having a hissy fit
Drenched as a drum
On our way to the playground while
My teacher puts on lipstick and perfume.

Zainab Rukhsar (9)
Moorlands School, Luton

Alien Journey

I went in my pink rocket,
Out to space.
But the fuel was quite down, low.
We popped into Mars to find some fuel.
Instead we saw an alien who mooed
The alien was quite rude
So we went out of there.

We saw some flashing lights,
Pink, red and green
But the aliens in there were very, very mean.
The aliens were dancing to the beat
So we said, 'Bye-bye' and we will soon meet again.

Roshni Patel (8)
Moorlands School, Luton

The Haunted House

The haunted house is a house of doom
Where witches brew potions
And ride on their brooms.
There are monsters that will chomp you,
Bit by bit.

Run! Run!
Away from your doom,
Turn around there's a headless groom,
Pianos' white keys flying around,
Something's behind you without a sound.
Finally you find the back door,
You open it and scream some more!

Anson Chan (10)
Moorlands School, Luton

Space Travel

Motor's running, countdown now 10, 9, 8, 7, 6, 5, 4, 3, 2, 1
Blast off, control system running,
Oh no! Low on fuel, it's gonna explode.
My rocket is going to crash on Mars. *Crash!*
What? I made the other astronaut,
Unconscious, what am I going to do?

Oh no! Strange creatures, what am I to do?
Here they come.
'Hello, we want to eat you.'
'Argh!'
I have to run!
Game over.

Robert Hussein (8)
Moorlands School, Luton

Travel To Space

3 . . . 2 . . . 1 . . . off!
We're going to space,
We're going to space.
Wait, the rocket's got no fuel,
How are we flying?
How are we flying?
I don't know,
I don't know.
Oh no!
We're about to crash.
Hold on, where's my sandwich.
Wait a minute, we're just in a toy rocket.

Sujay Chakrabarty (9)
Moorlands School, Luton

My Rocket Day

My rocket is very, very big!
One day I went to space in it,
Then someone lit a fire,
We were scared until I saw a tyre.

And I touched it, the rocket ran out of fuel,
And then suddenly I needed the loo,
Then suddenly I heard a moo,
And then an explosion!

Then the instruments failed,
We were landing on Earth,
So from that day, we never went on a rocket again.

Abhijay Malviya (9)
Moorlands School, Luton

Travelling To The Tudor Times

Travelling through Tudor times was really weird,
I saw a man with a banana beard.

Anne Boleyn had her head chopped off,
I saw someone making a paper cloth,
I got shipwrecked on a beach,
I had to clutch onto a piece of wood,
I swam back to shore,
I heard a knock at the door!

Jane Seymour died, Catherine Parr survived,
Henry VIII fought a war,
I thought he was a bore!

Carys Larne Stephens (9)
Moorlands School, Luton

The Knight

Sword wielder
Sword swinger
Throat cutter
Castle liver
Castle guarder
Bow shooter
Brain slicer
Shield holder
Heart slicer
Death striker.

Louis Brain (8)
Moorlands School, Luton

Cats

Milk drinker
Friend maker
Rolls over
Plays together
Walks calmly
Food eater
Furry creature
Nice animal
Tuna muncher
Biscuit eater.

Alisha Rauf (8)
Moorlands School, Luton

Fidgety Fish

Great wrigglers
Fast swimmers
Nice pets
Rock suckers
Shiny scales
Tall fins
Bright scales
Bubble blowers
Funny chaps
Strong swimmers.

Aena Noonari (8)
Moorlands School, Luton

Football

Goal scorers
Professional players
Fit players
Bad players
Poor referees
Nice goals
Yellow and
Red card
Dirty play
Cool stadiums.

Joseph Bradwell (8)
Moorlands School, Luton

Cheetah

Fast runner
Good catcher
High jumper
Sneaky runner
Vicious hunter
Fish eater
Eye lover
Good growler
Meat eater
Bone lover.

Ehsaan Mujahid (8)
Moorlands School, Luton

Stars

Stars, stars, wonderful things;
Shining in the violet-coloured sky;
Twinkling silently while the night goes by;
They sparkle in the distance, near and far;
That's why stars are wonderful things.

Stars, stars, wonderful things;
Shimmering like tiny dancers in the evening light;
The little stars shine so bright;
That's why stars are wonderful things.

Gwen Mei Scott (9)
Moorlands School, Luton

Monopoly

Game player
Winning player
Super player
Giving money
Getting money
Losing money
Buying houses
Buying hotels
Board game!

Alex Yip (7)
Moorlands School, Luton

Predators

P eering around the corner
R elying on his prey
E ngaging his lethal weapon
D estroying everything in the way
A mazing claws
T reats for him all around
O bserving you
R unning at high speed
S pine-chilling scariness.

Dimitrios Galatas (10)
Moorlands School, Luton

Flame

Flame is fierce and aggressive
Flame is a dragon and impressive
He flies across New York City
But no one sees him - such a pity.

Milen Patel (10)
Moorlands School, Luton

4M Class

In my class there's a wonky desk
In my class there's a broken chair
In my class there's a clock that smells
My friends have ripped up shorts
My friends have broken books
My desk has a broken hole
The wall has a crack next door
On the edge on the right
There's a box that smells.

Ellie Dudley (8)
Moorlands School, Luton

Love

Once there was a girl called Love
Who was as graceful as a dove,
She slipped on a woodlouse
And sadly never came out of the house.

She cried, she shouted,
But her mother doubted,
She didn't care!
Her family said she was rare!

Sristhi Agarwal (10)
Moorlands School, Luton

Dogs

Big licker
Great friend
Furry creature
Smelly pooper
Good runner
Sleepy sleeper
Actively fit
Always loving.

Jadesayo Ajibola (8)
Moorlands School, Luton

My Family

I'm very happy
And so is my dog happy,
My grandma can get quite nippy,
While my brother is a great big hippy.
My dad is really fab,
But the clothes he wears are rags!
Shame about my mother
All she does is hover!

Tremayne Barker (10)
Moorlands School, Luton

Dinner Ladies

If you're feeling like you need a munch,
Ask the dinner ladies for some lunch,
They prepare the food for you,
And some yummy puddings too
The dinner ladies are sweet,
They will give you a treat.

Sapphire Chapman (7)
Moorlands School, Luton

Artistic

A rt is so fun
R eal rushed painting
T ry new models
I love colouring
S cissors cutting
T he teacher is so kind
I love art
C hatting to friends.

Humaira Choudhary (9)
Moorlands School, Luton

Dancing

D elicious music
A stounding moves on the floor
N ewest dancers dancing
C razy men going mad
I t comes so instantly, you can't resist
N ow's the time to go, let's have a disco
G etting into your gear is such *fun!*

Elise Crick (9)
Moorlands School, Luton

Winter

Winter, winter, I love it so
Icicles hanging from my window
Snow falling on my face, as I build a snowman
'Don't forget to wrap up warm!' Mum shouts out.
All of the animals are hibernating until
The sun comes out in spring.
That is why I love winter.

Ingabelle Cole (10)
Moorlands School, Luton

In A Galaxy, Far, Far Away . . .

I am in space
Floating around happily
Slowly lunging into the heavy air
I wonder . . . who is out there?

All around me . . .
Comets . . . stars . . . planets . . . gazing at me,
Journeying steadily . . . constantly captured
In the sun's lasso.

All around me . . .
Unfamiliar aromas surround the senses.
Breathing in heavily, the senses are alert . . .
Stimulated by the mysterious fragrances of frankincense and myrrh

All around me . . .
Touching the ground
Silky and smooth
Touching and surrounded by rocks
Lost in this amazing world . . .

All around me . . .
The sounds of gulls crying
The sound of the shrieking of the falcon echoes in my head
Hearing the voices of humans below
Down on Earth . . . Our friends on Earth

All around me . . .
My time has come
I must leave my beloved world
Although I will always remember . . .
Everyone will remember our solar system and our Earth
All around me . . .

Raman Aval
Oakfields Montessori School, Upminster

Space

I am an alien in space,
A different kind of place,
Look around me and see,
The very empty scene,
What a place space can be.

The hot blazing sun,
That cannot be diminished,
What a place space can be.

Jupiter, Saturn and Uranus too,
Neptune and Pluto, we cannot see you,
These are nine planets that we know,
Round and round the sun they go,
What a place space can be.

Stephanie Talata Adongo (11)
Oakfields Montessori School, Upminster

I'm An Alien

I'm an alien and d'you know what.
I live on Mars and me name is Spot,
Me face is yellow and me hair is blue,
Me lips are purple and me spit is goo!

I'm an alien and d'you know what.
Me body's all green but me toes are not,
Me toes are smelly, they're red and pink,
And when I walk along I leave a terrible stink!

I'm an alien, and d'you know what,
I live on Mars and me name is Spot,
And as I look into the purple sky,
I think it's time to say goodbye.

Luke Spencer-Smith
Oakfields Montessori School, Upminster

Tutankhamun

T utankhamun died suddenly in 1327BC in the 9th year of his reign
U ndiscovered knowledge
T reasures of the tomb
A ntechamber - storing his treasure for the life beyond
N ew secrets revealed to the world
K illed pharaohs lying dead in the tombs
H oward Carter, the archaeologist who discovered it all
A khenaton was the father of Tutankhamun
M arried to his half-sister - Ankhesenamun
U nwrapping the mummy and that historical information that lay within
N efertiti was the mother of Tutankhamun.

Ria Gill (11)
Oakfields Montessori School, Upminster

Stars And Planets

S upernova stars exploding throughout the night
O ur star is the first star you will see tonight
L uminating the blackened sky at night
A steroid and meteoroids: vast lumps of rock
R oller coasting their way up and down until they have to stop.

S aturn has shining rings of light
Y ou will love to ride in a rocket to space at night
S ome are far into the galaxy, I want to be a star shimmering lovely
T he moon lights up the world at night
E arth is the colour of the deep blue sea
M y very educated mother just severed up Nandos for tea.

Bethany Ann Bradley (11)
Oakfields Montessori School, Upminster

Space

Space is like a playing field,
Each blade of grass is a planet
And each flower is a star.
The rain is the asteroids
And the children are the aliens,
So loud and noisy.
Space is a *big* place,
Just like my playing field.
If my field is *big,*
Space must be *gigantic!*

Ali Ahmad
Oakfields Montessori School, Upminster

The Sun

The sun is the best, the best of them all,
It lights up the world and keeps us all warm.
What else could there be to make us all happy?
I don't know what, it could be my daddy.
So many things wow my mind
Like the bright, bright sun, deep in the sky.
I have got to know if there are other planets,
I know what I'll do, ask my friend Janet.

Mia Choudhury
Oakfields Montessori School, Upminster

Pyramids

P yramids were built by slaves
Y oung and old
R un, hurry up!
A ngry pharaoh is coming
M ummies were put in pyramids
I t took 5000 men!
D ig, dig, dig
S ame as always!

Aleena Mirza
Oakfields Montessori School, Upminster

Planets!

Mercury - the marvellous messenger of the Romans!
Venus - the sweet goddess of love!
Earth - the life form planet!
Mars - the fiery, furious god of war!
Jupiter - the king of planets!
Pluto - the Roman name of the god Hades!

Nathan Dowdall (10)
Oakfields Montessori School, Upminster

Mummy

M ummies covered in bandages
U ncovering the secrets of the ancient world
M ummy's organs in a jar
M ummy's servants have been hurled
Y um, they say, bugs come from near and far.

Jorge Skinner
Oakfields Montessori School, Upminster

I Saw A Jolly Baker!

I saw a jolly baker,
Baking jolly bread,
He went out to the garden,
With flour on his head.

While inside the bakery,
His bread had turned to dust,
And over in the corner
Sat a jolly crust.

The baker smelt the burning,
And found to his surprise,
His bread was turning black,
Before his very eyes.

He turned off the oven,
And screamed out loud,
He had failed the baker test,
And he wasn't very proud.

I saw a jolly baker,
Baking no more bread,
The tester came to test it,
But the jolly baker fled!

Emily Lampon (10)
Rickling CE Primary School, Saffron Walden

Premier League!

Happy Hammers
Singing Sunderland
Heroic Hull
Pressure Portsmouth
Amazing Arsenal
Awesome Aston Villa
Super Spurs
Fantastic Fulham
Battering Bolton
Winning Wolves
Mad Man U
Burning Birmingham
Chilling Chelsea
Boring Burnley
Tricky Toffees
Living Liverpool
Surprising City
Blue Blackburn
Worrying Wigan.

Alfred Clark (9)
Rickling CE Primary School, Saffron Walden

Eiffel Tower

Once upon a time in France,
A person had a time,
When he saw a giraffe,
And thought,
Why don't we have a
Tower like that?
Because his name was Eiffel Tower,
Guess what
He called it that.

Julia Wasilewska (10)
Rickling CE Primary School, Saffron Walden

T-Rex

Meat seeker
Dino chaser
Night creeper
Roar talker
Tail whipper
Egg protector
Leaf shredder
Feet stomper
Den sleeper
Teeth chomper
Claw spreader
Pterodactyl taster
Human destroyer
Day danger

So: you've not even see a T-rex?

Nick Joannou (10)
Rickling CE Primary School, Saffron Walden

Mountain

On the great tall mountain
Where the snow lay
People played
People skied
People were snowboarding
That sounds fun!

Then people played in the snow
And the skiers skied
And people threw snowballs
In the sun
In the snow!

Louis Martin (9)
Rickling CE Primary School, Saffron Walden

The Sky Is Crying

The sky is crying, no one
Can stop it for its love
Is down below.

Find the heart
That lies shivering
And still beneath the
Sea of frozen waters.

Sadness is all you can see
There you shall see a shell full of love
The heart that belongs to the sky,
Now the sky is happy
And so is everyone, even
God Himself.

Faye Lyons (10)
Rickling CE Primary School, Saffron Walden

My Dream

As I lay asleep in my bed scary things run through my head,
Dreams of monsters, giants and witches too,
If you had those dreams would you wake up with a fright
And hear the storm and the thunder crashing down on
That dark night?
You lay down and fall asleep, you think you hear screams,
Children running but it's all just a dream.

My dream, my dream

My dream.

Rosie-Anna Reddey (9)
Rickling CE Primary School, Saffron Walden

Fantastic Fire-Breather

Ever heard of a crystal-protector?
Never heard of a fire-ejector?
Ever glimpsed a night-seeker?
Never rested with a cave-sleeper?
Ever observed a wing-spreader?
Never witnessed a person-shredder?
Ever read about a sky-matcher?
Never came across a claw-catcher?
So you've never seen a dragon?

Grace Leahy (10)
Rickling CE Primary School, Saffron Walden

'What Shall I Do?' I Said

'What shall I do?' I said
'Shall I climb a tree or bake some bread?
What shall I do?' I said
'My hair's falling out and it's time to go to bed.
Shall I make a mad invention and get a lot of attention?
Should I cry my eyes out or should I jump with glee?
        'What shall I do?' I said.

Eliza Parry Williams (10)
Rickling CE Primary School, Saffron Walden

Our Terror Had Begun

A drone of an engine,
A speck in the sky,
Then we knew we all could die.

Shatter of glass,
Then we run,
Our terror had just begun.

Flames were leaping,
Prancing around,
All there was, an eerie sound.

The sky became death,
Lit up red,
I was curled up, scared in bed.

Fear was twinkling,
In everyone's eyes,
We were as vulnerable as flies.

The bombs dropped
We heard a roar,
My heart being devoured by the war.

'Be safe'
My father had said
It kept echoing inside my head.

Tears of anger,
Rolled down my cheek,
My brother lay there cold and weak.

Death came quick,
Stabbed me like a knife,
I kissed goodbye to my life.

Lucille Corby (11)
St Anne's CE Primary School, Godmanchester

Remember

Remember, remember the 14th of November,
When at dusk Coventry was bombed,
The skies were misty from the flames of the city.

Remember, remember the 14th of November.
When the sirens were sounding,
People were dying, people were crying,
But there was nothing we could do.

Remember, remember the 14th of November,
When Anderson shelters were full,
The air raid helpers could not aid,
All were tired and all were thin.

Remember, remember the 14th of November,
Bombs were dropping,
Roads were flattened,
Buildings were crushed to the ground.

Remember, remember the 14th of November,
Homes were destroyed,
Everyone was annoyed,
Then finally came the fall of St Michael's Cathedral.

Nathan Brook (11)
St Anne's CE Primary School, Godmanchester

The Blitz

The shops are 'more open than usual',
Broken glass crunches under my feet.
A stench of fear engulfs the city,
Crawling through every street . . .

On the night of the moonlight sonata,
It is very cold and there's a full moon.
The siren sounds at ten past seven,
Take cover, the raid starts soon!

Fright creeps through my body;
I freeze as I hear another bomb sound.
Praying it isn't us next,
While a building crashes to the ground.

Somehow, we've made it to the morning,
The scene becomes clear as the dawn breaks above.
We are the only survivors, crying quietly,
For the loss of the ones we love.

Molly McKie (10)
St Anne's CE Primary School, Godmanchester

Daddy's War

Mummy sings a lullaby,
Lighting up the morning sky,
Glass crunching under feet,
Waving to people in the street.

All the children crying,
Lots of soldiers dying,
My daddy's fighting in the war,
I just wish he was safe at home once more.

Taylor Wilsher (11)
St Anne's CE Primary School, Godmanchester

Moonlight Sonata

The sky is inky black,
The full moon ahead,
Moonlight Sonata,
Soon I will be dead!

As I run through the streets,
The glass crunching under my feet,
I hear terrified screaming,
There's death at every street.

The bombs start to fall,
The fire rises up,
I watch people's fate,
It's getting rather late!

The bombs are coming closer,
I huddle up high,
But I cannot hide,
It's time for me to die.

Nicola Finch (10)
St Anne's CE Primary School, Godmanchester

WWII Child!

Screams are all around me,
But there's nothing I can see,
I'm trapped under heavy rubble,
And I can tell we're all in trouble.

The bomb went off so fast,
I know it's in the past.
All I feel is the rain,
And I feel I'm going insane.

The bomb that hit my shelter,
Was dropped by a German bomber.
Now I'm stuck under here,
With my eyes full of fear.

I am gasping for my last breath,
I feel I am very close to death,
Who will come to save me?
Who can set me free?

Amber Liddiard (11)
St Anne's CE Primary School, Godmanchester

WWII Nurse

Soldiers calling out mothers' and children's names,
Flesh burned and battered from the flames,
As the moon rises in the sky,
I know that patients are going to die.

Screams echoing off the hospital walls,
My hands are trembling as another bomb falls,
It feels like it is raining death,
As I hold the hand of a man who takes his last breath.

Tears welling up in my eyes,
Soldiers bandaged up, I hardly recognise,
A nurse's job is never done,
But I know the moonlight sonata has just begun.

Aimee Vale (10)
St Anne's CE Primary School, Godmanchester

This Is Not Right!

The moonlight sonata has begun,
Get in your shelters everyone,
My heart is thumping, my helmet heavy,
This is bad enough already!

I am worrying about my family at home,
Are my children all alone?
I have a job to do and must stay strong,
I must not break down, I must go on!

The booming sound,
As the bomb hits the ground,
Gives you a tremendous fright,
Why is this happening? This is not right!

Abie Whitehead (10)
St Anne's CE Primary School, Godmanchester

The Moonlight Sonata

Parachute flares like a giant fire starter
Were the opening chords of the moonlight sonata,
I could hear people crying in fear and in pain,
With incendiary bombs falling like rain.

Down in the shelter I felt so alone,
Listening to nothing, but the far distant drone,
The 'bombers moon' shone in the sky like a light,
My friends and my family may die in this fight.

St Michael's Cathedral was hit, what a pity,
After centuries standing guard over the city,
I tightened my scarf and put on my coat,
As the 'all clear' proclaimed the sonata's last note.

Joshua Clarke (10)
St Anne's CE Primary School, Godmanchester

Having Good Friends

My friends are always there!
We have marvellous times,
They play with me,
Help me,
Look after me
My friends are important,
And always stick up for me.
They come to my house
When I invite them,
They make me laugh!
They go shopping with me,
Whenever I'm scared they're there
Because they care!

My friends are brilliant!

Sophie Keal (10)
St Felix Junior School, Southwold

Will I Do This?

My dream is to stand on that block and hear the noise
of the gun
I wait patiently and nervously all at the same time
for the sound of the gun
I hear it and I pull myself back to get the most push I can get
I need to be streamlined
I need to be quick
I need to be first
I must kick
I must kick harder
I feel myself push into the wall and I am on my way back,
And I know I must kick harder if my dream is to come true
I have to be first
Only first
I need to have my dream come true
What is my dream?
My dream is to swim at an Olympic pool as an Olympic swimmer
As I kick as hard as I can I wonder, *will I be first or is my dream
not going to come true?*
I must not breathe for the last five metres.
It is the most Important five metres of my life
Have I got there? Am I first?
I look up and I see it - I am first
I am going to the Olympics!
My dream has come true.

Amelia Heard (10)
St Felix Junior School, Southwold

Swimming Through The Water

S moothly gliding through the water
W ater gushing past me
I 'm floating into a tumble turn
M oving slowly
M um watching on the balcony above
I 'm thinking how many lengths I've got left
N othing to do, just wondering what the time is
G o, go! Faster, sprint to the end

T hen turn to the side and breathe
H urrying, going fast to finish
R ushing, then stop
O nly 30 minutes left, yes!
U p and out to get my kick board
G et back in then push off the wall
H appy that it is breaststroke kick

T raining as hard as I can
H urrying to take over Emily, then I'm at the end
E veryone is glad when the teacher mentions it's swimdown!

W e are on the last 50 metres
A t last it's time to get out!
T ired, wanting to get home as fast as I can
E veryone is dressed and getting their shoes on
R ushing to get in the car, then I go home!

Sophie Bowler (10)
St Felix Junior School, Southwold

Robin In Reach Of My Hand

Little robin in the garden,
Flying around so innocently,
He has the most beautiful feathers,
The most dazzling red chest,
He glides so firmly,
He turns with a passion.
I sprinkle some seeds on the lawn,
Hoping he will enjoy them,
He pecks at the seeds,
One after the other,
He eats them so fast,
Within a blink of his beady eye . . . gone,
He was in reach of my hand,
I could touch him,
His wings flap,
Quicker and quicker they get,
He takes off like a gust of wind,
He is miles away from me now,
I didn't want any stunning robin to leave so soon,
Further and further and further . . .
My robin gets smaller,
As he drifts off into the distance.

Sophie Bodmer (10)
St Felix Junior School, Southwold

My Pet Dog, Arthur

A is for Arthur, my lovely pet dog
R is for run, he loves to do it a lot
T is for his toys, he loves to play with them
H is for home, he loves that the best
U is for understanding the signals I give him
R is for reliable, my lovely pet dog, Arthur.

Crystal Ellis (10)
St Felix Junior School, Southwold

Dotty The Pouncing Pup

It's Dotty's first walk,
Her little paws squelching through the soggy field,
She quivers for a moment,
She hears something,
A bird,
Now this is a *must have item* for Dotty.
Increasing in speed,
She runs up to the bird,
But not too close,
Dotty pauses . . .
She creeps,
Closer, closer
         And
            Closer
She pounces onto it
The bird is shocked
Success,
Well not for Dotty,
She missed,
And the bird has escaped . . .
And once again Dotty's jaws are empty.

Jessica Westlake (11)
St Felix Junior School, Southwold

The Medieval

Medieval
Historic, ancient
Chopping, terrifying, frightening
Spears, swords, inventions, technology
Ending, advancing, floating
Hi-tec, new
Future.

Logan Moore (11)
St Felix Junior School, Southwold

London

Giant, impressive buildings everywhere,
Hustling, bustling people going places,
Excited children staring around,
Tourists exploring this amazing city.
Look!
Over there, the London Eye,
Turning round slowly . . .
Watching over the city,
There's Big Ben standing ringing out his bell,
Buckingham Palace,
With its guards marching around.
Trafalgar Square with its magnificent
Statues and fountain,
And the lions guarding the square.
More sights to see,
Lots more places to discover.
But now we have to flag down a taxi,
To go now and catch a train.
I'm feeling sad about having to go,
From such an excellent day
In London.

Rose Heslin (11)
St Felix Junior School, Southwold

Doggy Days

Out in my garden I play with my pet
She likes to dig up the flower beds
In my house I play with my pet
She likes to be tickled on her tummy
Out on a walk I lead my dog
She likes to tug and tug but . . .
I still hang on.

Sarah Watts (10)
St Felix Junior School, Southwold

The Nut Is On The Loose!

Fast runner,
Nut cracker,
Swift mover,
Cuddly climber,
Fluffy thinker,
Tree climber,
Speedy catcher,
Silent thinker,
Prompt jumper,
Crazy hunter,
Sharp cracker,
Quick hider,
Gentle burier,
Sudden climber,
Good thinker,
Dashing robber,
Warm whiskers,
Golden thinker,
Rapid hunter.

The squirrel!

Emma French (10)
St Felix Junior School, Southwold

Night - Day

Night
Black, dark
Screaming, creeping, shining
Shadow, darkness, brightness, sparkle
Shimmering, daylight, glowing
Sunny, light
Day.

Matthew Magson (10)
St Felix Junior School, Southwold

My Baby Brother, Will

First day home he's red and small
Now today two feet tall
Second day home he cries and eats
Now today he likes rock beats.
Third day he's sick everywhere
Now today he has some hair.
Fourth day home he smiles a bit
Now today he can sit.
Fifth day home he dribbles and smells
Now today he claps and tells.
Sixth day home he starts to sleep
Now today he tries to leap.
Seventh day home I love him to bits
Even though he cries,
Eats,
Is sick,
Dribbles
And smells
I love him just as well!

Georgie Hazelgrove (11)
St Felix Junior School, Southwold

The Fox

Night stalker
Fantastic hunter
Silent pouncer
Rabbit murderer
Hare killer
Loving howler
Wonder bringer
Beautiful seeker
Scary taker.

Arna Tolliday (10)
St Felix Junior School, Southwold

My Pink Cat

My bold cat makes quite a statement
As he meanders through town,
Showing off his sparkling new coat
Not paying attention to anything except himself.
Lurching his long tail like a snake
He halts at a puddle.
Staring at his reflection
Checking out his coat
His bright pink coat.
Making people gaze at the sight
Off he plods, glaring at the sky.
Thump . . .
There's a booming cry of laughter,
Rushing over
Worrying,
I pick him up
     Phew
          He's alright!

Alexandra Paulley (11)
St Felix Junior School, Southwold

Future Weapons

Future weapons are being adapted.
Taliban hiding among innocent people.
Rocket launchers and howitzers firing.
Helicopters dropping troops and firing.
IEDs on the roadsides
Explosions and fire.
Tanks and buffaloes.
Mines don't harm them.
The enemy attack, throwing grenades.
Down go the Taliban.

Harvey Catchpole (9)
St Felix Junior School, Southwold

Sad Ending

17 years of age
My gorgeous little pussy cat.
He hates the vet
But he has to go!
For ten minutes we wait . . .
As we go through our hearts are racing
While he's checking up.
He finds a problem.
'I would like to take some blood,' he says
He arrives back, he tells us the problem,
His kidneys are failing
He'll have to go on a diet
And have to have a pill every day.
When we arrive home
There's a phone call from the vet
Harley could live up to a month
Or a year . . .
Then we all start crying.

Rosie Kinsella (10)
St Felix Junior School, Southwold

Wolf Comes

W hen you see a wolf mind out where you step
O n the plains of the forest
L iving in the depths
F ind yourself in danger

C oming to get you
O n the hunt
M ore and more are coming
E nding now . . . you're gone
S creaming through the night.

Brooke Smith (11)
St Felix Junior School, Southwold

Purr . . . Purr . . . Purr . . . !

Purr . . . purr . . . purr . . . says my cat
My cat at home is innocent, always purring and eating food
But what does he do when I'm not there?
Killer . . . ?
Burglar . . . ?
Well what is he?
When he comes in he's shedding blood,
In his back pocket there is a gun.
Charlie!
You human murderer
You bad boy!
But on the floor in front of him
There is a rabbit with a toy gun in his fur
Then we go back to
Purr . . .
Purr . . .
Purr . . .

Jack Fuller (10)
St Felix Junior School, Southwold

Mind Drifting

The teacher is so boring today,
My mind starts drifting . . .
The roof goes back,
I zoom into the distance,
The wind is blowing in my face,
The fluff on the steering wheel is tickling my hands,
The wheels are spinning,
The seats are as soft as bubbles,
Passing lorries, vans and cars,
I screech to a halt,
I'm in my lime-green mini.

Isobel Knowles (11)
St Felix Junior School, Southwold

Safest Place

The rhythm of endless years,
The beat of a thousand tears.
I ponder upon how many places the sea has been . . .
How many faces has it seen?
Yet still,
It's so lonely,
So isolated,
So alone.
It cries out in a wailing,
Weeping tone.
I find peace and serenity in the sea,
I feel as though nothing can hurt or upset me.
Nothing more,
Nothing less,
The safest place in the world for me . . .
The sea.

Rosy Kelvey (11)
St Felix Junior School, Southwold

Seas Of The World

The sea never ends,
The blinding waters of the Pacific,
Where it's so deep its bed never comes,
The freezing waters of the Atlantic,
Where the sunken ship of the Titanic lies,
The seas of the world are,
Beautiful
Wonderful
And a terrific
Place
To
Be.

Samuel Ellis (10)
St Felix Junior School, Southwold

Naughty Food

Ice cream yum in my tum,
Cold and icy on my tongue.

Yummy sweets hard and chewy,
Chomp, chomp, chomp,
My teeth are all gooey.

Yummy cake soft and spongy,
With icing on the top.

All these things aren't good for you,
If you have a lot.

All this naughty food,
I have written about,
I could not live without.

May Bandy (10)
St Felix Junior School, Southwold

Life Stories

I think life is great
Just because everyone's different.
You might be tall,
You may be small
It doesn't really matter
It's just the way you are.
You might be slim,
You might be fat,
You might be in the middle.
You might be disabled
But don't think that you're different
Just because you look different
We're all the same inside.

Ross Tolliday (9)
St Felix Junior School, Southwold

Holly

Holly is my springer spaniel
She is eleven years of age
And she is very energetic.
She loves to run and jump about
But she hates the sound of gunshots.
When she sees a rabbit she chases it away.
Holly loves to go on walks.
She gets very sad if she does not have one.
And she starts to beg
Eventually I give in!
Holly is the best dog
Nothing will ever replace her.

Kyle Coles (10)
St Felix Junior School, Southwold

The Future

The future was so cool
Bit of a shame it was run by a fool.

The future was so bright
But if you go there you will have a bit of a fright.

Looked like the staff had made their cars,
Out of rusty, old, rotten stars.

The buildings were so high,
You could look over the sky.

What I ate for lunch,
Was a chocolate robot crunch.

Daniel Martin (11)
St Felix Junior School, Southwold

My Pony

Early in the morning I run to my pony's stable,
When he hears my footsteps
He trots to his stable door
Neighs for his food
He loves honey chop, nuts, sugarbeet and pulse mix
Out of all my horses he likes food the best!
He enjoys his hacks and likes jumping too
On our first show together
Nokie won two trophies and three rosettes!
He was excellent.
I love my pony to pieces.

Imogen Templer (9)
St Felix Junior School, Southwold

Ginger, My Chicken

Ginger is the best chicken in the land.
She's the only hen who lays eggs in my hand!
She can balance on my arm, even on my back.
That's because she trusts me,
Her feathers are gingery brown.
She goes crazy for the food she wants.
Ginger is the best chicken in the universe!

Archie Wallis (10)
St Felix Junior School, Southwold

Morning · Night

Morning
Restful, relaxed
Eating, sleeping, resting
Lay-in, TV, bath, computer
Facebooking, partying, joking
Fun, joyful
Night.

James Sutton (11)
St Felix Junior School, Southwold

Sweets

S is for sweets
W is for weep when you do not get them
E is for the enjoyment of having them
E is for the experience of eating them
T is for teeth, too many are bad for them
S is for sticky, like they make your fingers.

Oliver Chantry (10)
St Felix Junior School, Southwold

Hector

H ector has ears like carpet slippers
E yes like blackberries
C ute fat paws which leave muddy footprints everywhere
T eeth like tiny daggers
O bviously the cutest thing in existence
R unning around like a wild thing!

Annabel Hood (11)
St Felix Junior School, Southwold

Larry

L is for lazy Larry who sleeps all day
A is for appetite for chicken food
R is for Larry ruining things!
R is for running around like a headless cockerel!
Y is for yummy food he pecks.

Archie Laughland (10)
St Felix Junior School, Southwold

The Seaside

At the seaside you will see lots of people eating ice cream,
Watching the sea clash on the shore,
Eating chips and fresh fish that we adore,
Lovely days, sunny and bright at the seaside,
Before our dark, black night.

At the seaside you will see seagulls flying over the sea,
Buckets and spades to play with every day on the sand,
Seeing ships come into a port,
The fish in the sea go *bubble, bubble, bubs,*
Before our dark, black night.

At the seaside you will see sandy beaches,
Soft and crumbly like a piece of snow,
Sand everywhere, oh what we adore,
Sand oh yes, sandy and more,
Before our dark, black night.

At the seaside you will see waves on the sandy shore,
Clashing and bashing,
Also the waves swim in the deep blue sea just like busy bumblebees
Fishy fish swim all day in the deep blue sea
Before our dark, black night.

Charley Edgar (10)
St James CE (VA) Middle School, Bury St Edmunds

Crawling, Crawling

The man crawled,
Alone,
Always alone,
He crawled to escape,
Escape the claws of death,
He crawled to hide the body of
Failure,
To hide the shell he was trapped in,
A shell of fear,
A shell of shame.

The girl crawled,
Lonely,
Always lonely,
She crawled to survive,
Survive the attack strategies of
Death, itself,
She crawled to grab and reach at hope,
All hope,
Any hope.

The forbidding headlights of a car,
Penetrated their safety,
Penetrated the dark
They hid,
Or died.

Fear gripped them both like a hand,
Squeezing the air from them,
Stealing their life and hope,
They wished for the ground to
Swallow them up,
For the wet grass to hide their faces,
Hide their humiliation.

The headlights passed by again,
The man sunk lower into the ground,
The child stifled tears,
They hid,
Or died.

Tilly Dalglish (11)
St James CE (VA) Middle School, Bury St Edmunds

Butterfly

Butterfly, butterfly,
Fly up into the sky,
Fly up to the sky really high.
Meet lots of butterflies, play all day long.
Yellow, blue, red, pink, white,
And all sorts of colours.

When the nights come,
Be careful of butterfly Mary,
Because she is naughty.

Mary, Mary, stealing night,
What is going to happen tonight?
She steals lots of things.

Hide and say goodbye
In the early morning find some food,
Be in a good mood,
Play, play, play,
And be happy all day.

Misia Fajgier (10)
St James CE (VA) Middle School, Bury St Edmunds

Icicle

Wicked winter's frosty fingers
Steal all the leaves,
Scatters them around the ground
Yet only snow he leaves

Winter, wonder worker
Makes gleaming icicles hang,
He made the snow fall from the sky,
As the carollers sang.

Now back to the evil thief,
Blowing across the land.
He's realised he's got the weather
In the palm of his hand.

The wonder worker's proved to us,
That when there's no sun,
We can play around in snow,
And still have lots of fun!

Abigail Simpson (11)
St Mary's CE (VA) Primary School, Hadleigh

Winter

Winter ices the paths
Creating treachery and disaster
Icicles, sharp as a rapier,
Ready to strike.

Winter blasts pulsing blizzards
Making people stuck everywhere,
And making roads vulnerable.

Winter turning it as cold as the Arctic itself,
Now we must wait for spring
For it all to be over.

Harvey Mason (10)
St Mary's CE (VA) Primary School, Hadleigh

Winter Magician

W onderful winter world
I ced tree roots
N imble snow falling
T ingling snow falling
E choing snow caves
R aining storms of snow.

M agical icicles of trees
A bstract spiderwebs covered in snow
G limmers of light of icicles
I maginative winter world
C alm ice on trees
I cicle hands
A ffected feelings
N on negative.

Toby Emmerson (9)
St Mary's CE (VA) Primary School, Hadleigh

Weird Winter

Vital, numbing, sharp and bitter,
In the snow he puts some glitter,
He gets carried away putting out snow,
He absolutely hates it when it has to go,
He likes finding things just to kill,
And he makes some people very ill,
He gives the summer a lot of hate,
Because he thinks the freezing is so great,
Sometimes he makes it rain,
Just so he can see us complain,
With snow some people don't have to go to their schools,
That means a whole day with no school rules!

Oliver Smith (10)
St Mary's CE (VA) Primary School, Hadleigh

Winter

Winter ices the paths,
Creates danger and treachery.
Cars crash,
Blizzards blast across the country.

He has hidden the grass,
Below a magical, sparkling blanket,
He has frozen the lakes,
We can go ice skating!

Jay Collis (11)
St Mary's CE (VA) Primary School, Hadleigh

Winter

Glittering,
Riddling, puzzling,
Mysterious, magical, baffling,
Icicles, snowmen, crunching, bitter,
Bleak, murky, brutal,
Slippy, icy,
Gloomy.

Joel Simpson (11)
St Mary's CE (VA) Primary School, Hadleigh

Weird Times To Go To Bed

When it's winter I have to wake up at night.
I wonder why I have to wake up like that.
When it is summer, I have to sleep when it is still bright.
I hear grown-ups' feet stamping on the floor.

I wish I slept whenever I wanted.

Jordana Wong (9)
St Nicholas Priory Junior School, Great Yarmouth

Broken

Broken heart
Broken lance
Broken bone
You broke me.

Broken thought
Broken promise
Broken silence
Too much said.

Broken wing
Broken treaty
Broken arrow
Wasted chance.

Broken wing
Broken thoughts
Broken spirit
You're so mean.

Broken wing
Broken glass
Broken mirror
Seven days of bad luck.

Broken vow
Broken bow
Broken love
Alone again.

Broken words
Broken pencil
Broken drawer
I give up.

There's too much
Broken stuff.

Joel Moreira (9)
St Nicholas Priory Junior School, Great Yarmouth

All About My Dragon

My dragon knows . . .
How to eat horrible people
How to fly high in the sky
How to glide wicked like Concorde
How to blow blood high in the sky
How to be as strong as a dinosaur
How to make a person die
How to be disgusting in public
How to go to school
How to say sorry to someone
How to say goodbye
How to be helpful
How to be nice
How to say how nice you look today
How to run fast
How to dance and do ballet and gym
How to play football
How to not blow fire in the sky
How to say goodnight
How to get in a car
How to drive and not crash
How to be nice to everyone
How to get your anger out
How to know the time
How to turn the telly on
How to keep your room tidy
How to get into bed
How to play nice
How to drink
How to eat nicely in public
How to play the piano

Madelynn Bott (8)
St Nicholas Priory Junior School, Great Yarmouth

The Four Seasons

Winter
The temperature is so cold
In winter weather nobody's bold
Snow lays on the ground like it's at home
Igloos and snowmen shaped round like a dome.

Autumn
Leaves falling to the ground
It is not a very pleasant sound
Green turning to red and brown
The trees all frown.

Spring
My favourite time of the year
Filled with all the rabbits, birds and deer
Leaves start to grow back on the trees
Beautiful flowers packed with bees.

Summer
Children and families on the beach
With picnics including peach
Make sandcastles and play in the sea
You won't have to pay, it's all *free!*

Shelby Cox (10)
St Nicholas Priory Junior School, Great Yarmouth

Aladdin

Once there lived a boy,
Whose life had very little joy,
But then he met a lovely girl
Who wanted a very pretty pearl.

So then he took her home,
To brush her hair with a wooden comb
Then she met his pet monkey
And thought he was really funky.

Jafar tricked him
And pretended his name was Tim,
Aladdin went into a cave
Thinking he was really brave.

Then he met a genie,
Wearing a pink bikini,
Also a flying carpet with a spot
Aladdin liked it quite a lot.

Molly Hayes (9)
St Nicholas Priory Junior School, Great Yarmouth

What I Do At School

I walk across the playground at a marvellous pace,
But it still doesn't stop me from getting a ball in the face!
When I'm doing push-ups I try, try, try!
Although it makes me cry, cry, cry!
There has to be another way,
But I still have to clean out my tray.
Teachers don't think I'm cool when I'm in class acting the fool,
I think my school is the best,
But I enjoy the weekend to have a rest.
In golden time, I'm allowed to watch 'Thriller'
But missing it is a killer!

Kain McBarron (9)
St Nicholas Priory Junior School, Great Yarmouth

Baby Land

When she wasn't here,
The house was clear,
So tiny and small,
Will she ever grow tall?

We're glad she's here to make us smile,
We waited and waited for such a long while.

Her name is Frankie,
Sometimes she's a bit cranky,
She likes to have six bottles a day,
So she can grow strong and big enough to play.
She sleeps all day
She sleeps all night
We have to be quiet
So we don't give her a fright.

Shannon McMullan (10)
St Nicholas Priory Junior School, Great Yarmouth

Chocolate Land!

I live in Chocolate Land,
Everything is chocolate except your hand,
The sky is blue, the grass is brown,
But most of all nobody has a frown.
We have a chocolate park
The park keeper is called Mark,
The dogs are dark brown, the cats are white,
The best thing is it's always bright.
I have shown you the tour,
But I can't show you any more,
I hope you have enjoyed Chocolate Land,
Now please take this free bag of sand.

Blàz Freshwater (10)
St Nicholas Priory Junior School, Great Yarmouth

A Witch Outside My Window

There's a witch outside my window
She will not go away
There's a gremlin on my doorstep
And I think he's here to stay.

There's a troll demanding candy
And a mummy wanting sweets.
There's a ghost, a ghoul, a goblin,
And they're grumbling for treats,
And as it isn't another shocking Hallowe'en
And as scary as it sounds,
There is a witch in town.

Mellissa Stretton (10)
St Nicholas Priory Junior School, Great Yarmouth

One To Ten

Ten little girls walking in the park,
Nine little boys saying, 'Bark, bark, bark'
Eight tiny dogs barking at the tree
Seven stray cats purring at me.
Six cute puppies resting on their bed,
Five weird hamsters bumping their head.
Four huge lions laying on the grass,
Three ugly soldiers saying, 'You can't pass.'
Two cheeky monkeys jumping tree to tree,
One little girl writing a poem . . . That's *me!*

Daniela Alves (9)
St Nicholas Priory Junior School, Great Yarmouth

Animal Alphabet

A nimals are the best
B ees sting you if you hurt them
C ollars are for dogs
D ancing Dalmations
E xcellent elephants
F antastic fish
G iant giraffes
H unting dogs
I love penguins, they are so cool
J umping jellyfish
K angaroos in love
L eaping lions
M agic cats
N aughty elephants squirt water
O ctopus in the sea
P enguins need ice to live
Q ueen of the cheetahs
R unning tigers
S noozing caterpillars
T igers leaping up high
U nrolling hedgehogs
V ery fat cats
W hite and black Dalmatians
eX tinct dinosaurs
Y oung tiger cubs
Z ebras running!

Megan Utting (8)
Sextons Manor CP School, Bury St Edmunds

The Moon I Love

The moon I love so high above
Makes me feel so loved
That's the moon I love
Lots of fun so high above
Why can't I be there too?
I really wish I could
That's what I really want,
Don't you?
The moon is so bright
It fills me with delight,
And sometimes a little fright too
When the day is done
I have fun with the moon,
Until it fades away into another day
When I see the moon
I think it's
Really true
That's the moon I truly love.

Charlotte Marchment (8)
Sextons Manor CP School, Bury St Edmunds

The Magic Moon

Magic moon, magic moon, in the sky above
Magic moon, magic moon, you're the one I love
Magic moon, magic moon, are you fairy dust
Or are you just a big wind gust?
Magic moon, magic moon, you're big in the sky
Or are you wise and bright when you come to fly?
As the stars fly with you it reminds me
I have company too.
Magic moon, magic moon, in the sky above
Magic moon, magic moon, you're the one I love.

Alexandra Barnes (8)
Sextons Manor CP School, Bury St Edmunds

Shiny Little Moon

Shiny little moon
Come and shine on me
Let me shine as bright as you
Lift me up as high as you
So I can see space too.

Little moon, please let me
Go as high as you
Because I love space too.
I know you said I am
Too young but I am cute.

And when I am up in the sky
I will open my arms and legs
And close my eyes
So I look like a big star.

Sophie Strudwick (8)
Sextons Manor CP School, Bury St Edmunds

The Skeleton

T he longest bone is the femur
H umerus is the top arm bone
E yes are black in your skeleton.

S pine is made out of vertebrae
K nee caps (posh name is patella)
E lbow joint makes your hand hit your shoulder
L eg bones are fibula and tibia
E very day I use my bones
T here are 206 bones in your body
O h no, hope I don't break one
N o, I broke one!

Kian Neary (8)
Sextons Manor CP School, Bury St Edmunds

See The Moon

Why can't you see the moon?
I can, it's very bright and clear
Can't you see it dear girl?

It's very bright and white
It fills the sky and it's all brilliant.

What a lovely moon inside it
With a lovely cover.

Oh dear! You are so beautiful moon,
I don't know what to do!
Please help, I am so sad.

Paige Gaze (8)
Sextons Manor CP School, Bury St Edmunds

The Moon Shines

The moon shines so bright,
Brighter than ten stars.
It fills up all the ground
And everyone sees it at night,
Maybe morning.

The moon never dies,
It just keeps coming and never goes.
The sky is never dark,
The sun is different to the moon
Because it is like it's nocturnal.

Jordan Coe (7)
Sextons Manor CP School, Bury St Edmunds

Performing

P eople in the audience
E verybody clapping away
R eady to go on stage
F amous people like to go
O K, we're ready to go!
R eady when you are
M illions of people are going to watch me
I love to perform
N o I'm not scared
G reat - let's take a bow.

Molly Ann Owen (7)
Sextons Manor CP School, Bury St Edmunds

Mountains

M y top has got snow on it
O ut on the rainy days my snow turns to slush
U ntil the summer, that's when the slush melts
N ow people come to climb on me in the summer
T hen they get to the top
A nd they get back down
I t's night-time when I go to sleep
N ow ghosts fly round me
S ome day I will get to the top.

Lucien Edwards (7)
Sextons Manor CP School, Bury St Edmunds

Rainbows

R ainbows are colourful
A ll of the colours make me happy
I t is beautiful, my favourite colour's gold
N ew rainbows come and go
B lue is the best
O ut of the sky
W ow, rainbows fascinate me
S oon they have to go.

Jade Ellis (8)
Sextons Manor CP School, Bury St Edmunds

Insects

I tchy ants
N o legs on worms
S orry Mr Millipede
E very bee gets honey
C entipedes are orange
T ermites bite, really hard!
S o that proves there are different bugs on Earth.

Rowan Gibb (7)
Sextons Manor CP School, Bury St Edmunds

Horses

H orses are funny and cute
O ats are what they eat
R ide away and gallop like the wind
S addle up and ride!
E njoy riding on a horse
S tables are where you clean them.

Niamh Quinn (7)
Sextons Manor CP School, Bury St Edmunds

Flower

F loating petals on the ground
L ily petals like a floating sun in the air
O ak trees all around
W onderful whistling birds in your ear
E legant ladies walking across the park
R oses are red as a heart upon your head.

Emily Roach (8)
Sextons Manor CP School, Bury St Edmunds

The Great Man Came Riding
(Inspired by 'The Highwayman' by Alfred Noyes)

The great man came riding in the night
Holding tight,
Onto his horse which was not in sight,
Then he reached the great grand tree,
And next of course was the sea,
There he found Bess lying,
With blood all over,
Then he kissed her on the shoulder,
He stabbed himself in the head and then he was truly dead.

They both flew up to Heaven,
With angels above them,
They both imagined paradise
Which is of course nice.
But they still had that little horror in their head,
From when they dropped dead.

Yasmin Motarjemi (9)
Stapleford Community Primary School, Stapleford

169

A Night Of Gloom And Doom
(Inspired by 'The Highwayman' by Alfred Noyes)

The sea was a thousand horses;
Each with a tall white mane,
And all alone on the cliff top
A man rode on the cobbled lane.

His hair was sleek and black;
He had a purple coat, warm and long
And as he rode on the cliff top
He sang a simple song.

About his one love, the landlord's daughter,
Lily, with the beautiful auburn hair,
But this was a night of gloom and doom
So should he not beware?

Meanwhile Lily sat on her window sill waiting
When suddenly out of the light;
Tom the odd job man, looking up at her
It was love at first sight.

They reached out for each other,
When, *crack*, a bullet shot so fast,
From the rifle of Lily's fake true love,
Who had just seen what had passed.

Now he was livid,
He wanted blood, he wanted more and more
Oh yes he was angry,
But did he really want to go to war?

Again he shot, but his aim was bad,
And Lily was shot, through the head.
She fell into Tom's arms,
And there they lay, both dead.
And all of this happened on a night of gloom and doom.

Esmé Kovacs (9)
Stapleford Community Primary School, Stapleford

Under The Sea

Under the sea
Is the place to be,
You can swim with all the fishes,
Under the sea
Is the place for me,
Because mermaids grant your wishes.

Under the sea,
The deep blue sea,
You can swim with whales,
Under the sea,
The whale-filled sea,
Be careful of whales' tails!

Under the sea,
You can have tea,
With a starfish in the dark.
Under the sea,
The fun-filled sea,
Just beware of sharks!

Under the sea
Is the place to be,
You can swim with all the fishes.
Under the sea
Is the place for me,
Because mermaids grant your wishes.

Hannah Lin (9)
Stapleford Community Primary School, Stapleford

The Little Fish

I had this little fish
He was going to be on a dish
I put him under my shawl
And put him in a bowl
A bowl full of water
Then gave him to my daughter,
She loved him but then,
Served him in a tin,
So now that poor little fish
Is now on a dish
So I guess that little fish was meant to be
On a dish after all.
So today, on this very day in May
We celebrate the day that the fish on the dish is dead.

Sophie Challis (10)
Stapleford Community Primary School, Stapleford

The Planets

Mercury and Venus too
Jupiter and Mars
Come and be an astronaut
Reach for the stars
Saturn and Uranus
Pluto and Earth
Being an astronaut
Is as exciting as giving birth!
Neptune is very hot
But the sun is hotter
The sun shines on all the planets
Space is better than Harry Potter.

Áine Deane (9)
Stapleford Community Primary School, Stapleford

My Poem About A War Fighter Pilot

As I fly all around looking
For German planes that
Are hiding from us
So when we least expect it
They will shoot us down
Like little flies
I think about all the people
That are dying from the
Bombs that fall each night
Why don't the Germans go
Back to Germany where they
Belong and leave us in peace?
In England, there I spot a plane
Of the enemy,
Off my thoughts go
And enjoy the freedom of
Never being hurt and the
Worry of death, what is
The chance of that happening?
No chance at all.

Charlotte Baggaley (11)
The Cathedral CE (VA) Primary School, Chelmsford

Across The Road

Across the road is where happiness is
Across the road is where my friends are
Fame and fortune are all across that road
In the misty darkness is where I am crying out for help
No one else can help me, I must do this myself
When I reach my destination everything will be clear
Even though I am not there it's a better life over that road.

Erin Blunderfield (9)
The Cathedral CE (VA) Primary School, Chelmsford

To My Destination

The fish bubble, bubble, bubble
Jellyfish wobble, wobble, wobble
I float up high
Right to the sky
The birds tweet
There is a tingle in my feet
A cry of joy
Oh boy
What a day
Way hay
The grass waves behind me
There is a lot I can see
Cows eating
Smiling faces
Different places

What a day
I won't forget.

Pearl Bulgin (10)
The Cathedral CE (VA) Primary School, Chelmsford

ABC Of Travel

All the time I travel
By air, land or sea
Counting all the transport
Different or like me
Enjoying all the places
Far and near alike
Going round the cities
Hike or mountain bike
Identifying vehicles
Jumping out of planes
Kicking sand while walking
Lifting cars with cranes
Moving around the world
Never taking breaks
Over bridges high and low
Passing over lakes.

Eden Tanner (10)
The Cathedral CE (VA) Primary School, Chelmsford

Cool Camper Vans

C ool camper vans, travel on
A dventurous journeys around the world, their
M etal work shining in the blazing sun, colourful
P urple, or wacky designs, they
E xplore the countryside roaming the land
R ebel vans, they work night and day

V acations in the open air, with
A ctive people who love to share, the wonders of
N ature anywhere, in the vehicle that
S urfers love everywhere.

Naomi Hunt (11)
The Cathedral CE (VA) Primary School, Chelmsford

When I Bought My Cat A Present

I bought our cat a jetpack
Which I think she liked a lot.
She strapped it on and instantly
She took off like a shot.

She zoomed around my bedroom
Then she blasted down the hall.
She bounced off every piece
Of furniture and off every wall.

Our dog freaked out and ran away,
Our hamster squeaked and fled,
I even saw my sister hiding
Underneath her bed.

So don't make any mistake and give your cat a present,
Because all they'll want to do is blast off up to Heaven.

Abigail Hackett (10)
The Cathedral CE (VA) Primary School, Chelmsford

Perfect Pony

Noisy neigher
Graceful galloper
Top trotter
Clip clopper
Cool canterer
Joyful jumper
Dreamy dressager
Wacky walker
Eager eater
Drooly drinker
Excellent eventer
Groovy grazer
Fabulous friend!

Dulcie Livens (10)
The Cathedral CE (VA) Primary School, Chelmsford

Up And Away

H urry up, in the air I go
O ut of town and in the sky
T owards the clouds I float

A ngry fire takes me up and up
I look down to the town
R olling fields look so small

B irds glide past me
A ll around me is peace
L ovely, lovely quiet
L ovely and so still
O nwards I go off on my journey
O ff into the sky
N ow I am back down in town.

Erin Barker (11)
The Cathedral CE (VA) Primary School, Chelmsford

Sailing In The Wind

I'm flying in my hot air balloon,
I hope I'm not going to land too soon
As this is a wonderful sight
I'm glad I'm not scared of heights.

There's a place over there with lots of trees
And I'm being carried by the breeze,
I'm looking down at the seas,
Whilst gently hugging at my knees.

As I fly past amazing things,
Like a graceful bird with wonderful wings.
Nearly at my destination, it seems,
As the wind carries me in my dreams!

Nina Harrington (10)
The Cathedral CE (VA) Primary School, Chelmsford

Aeroplane · Haikus

Sky glider, flyer
Up above the clouds so high,
Holiday traveller.

Never stops for breaks
Working always, all the time
Over the ocean.

Taking off speedy
In the air, floating with clouds
Landing's just bizarre!

Alice Loughran (9)
The Cathedral CE (VA) Primary School, Chelmsford

Cornwall In The Spring

C an you see the squirrels scampering up the trees?
O range sunsets glow above the sea
R ainbows colour the sky
N ests are full of eggs hatching in the trees
W ading through the sea in wellingtons
A ll the birds are cheeping merrily
L ots of trees are blossoming
L ovely sunshine shines in the sky.

Cornwall is my favourite place to be.

Alexandra Gibson (10)
The Cathedral CE (VA) Primary School, Chelmsford

The Thing With Transport

Trains are a pain, even when it really rains
Cars won't go to Mars when you're eating chocolate bars
Planes can't go down lanes when you're eating candy canes
Bikes can't catch pikes when you're wearing stripy tights
Skates can't go over gates when you're running really late
So don't use these to get across seas!

Shannon Barnett (9)
The Cathedral CE (VA) Primary School, Chelmsford

Planes

High flyer
Passenger taker
Cloud plunger
Gentle lander
Crowd pleaser
World polluter
Fuel user.

Sophie McLellan (9)
Wicklewood Primary School, Wymondham

Young Writers Information

We hope you have enjoyed reading this book - and that you will continue to enjoy it in the coming years.

If you like reading and writing poetry drop us a line, or give us a call, and we'll send you a free information pack.

Alternatively if you would like to order further copies of this book or any of our other titles, then please give us a call or log onto our website at www.youngwriters.co.uk.

A platform for your poetry!

Young Writers Information
Remus House
Coltsfoot Drive
Peterborough
PE2 9JX
(01733) 890066

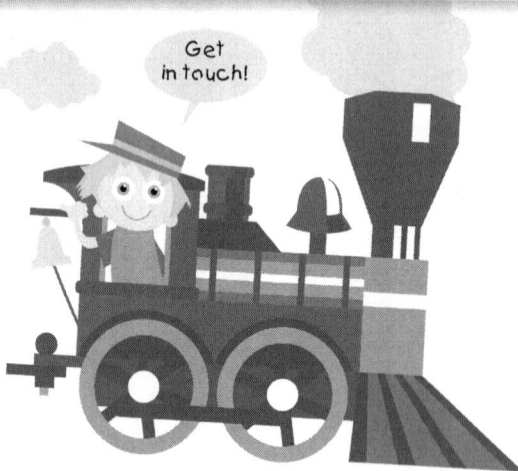

Get in touch!